THE OUTBREAK OF THE FIRST WORLD WAR

DATE DUE

MY 27 90		
OC 13 90		
NO 3 00		
OC 10 02		
DE 21 02		
DE 6 04		

Studies in European History

General Editor: Richard Overy
Editorial Consultants: John Breuilly
Roy Porter

PUBLISHED TITLES

FORTHCOMING

THE OUTBREAK OF THE
FIRST WORLD WAR

1914 in Perspective

DAVID STEVENSON
Senior Lecturer in International History
London School of Economics

A catalogue record for this book is available from the British Library.

ISBN 0–333–58327–2

First published in the United States of America 1997 by
ST. MARTIN'S PRESS, INC.,
Scholarly and Reference Division,
175 Fifth Avenue, New York, N.Y. 10010

ISBN 0–312–16539–0

Library of Congress Cataloging-in-Publication Data
Stevenson, D. (David), 1954–
The outbreak of the First World War : 1914 in perspective / David
Stevenson.
p.   cm. — (Studies in European history)
Includes bibliographical references and index.
ISBN 0–312–16539–0
1. World War, 1914–1918—Causes.   2. World War, 1914–1918—Europe.
I. Title.   II. Series : Studies in European history (New York, N.Y.)
D511.S817   1997
940.3'11—dc20   96–34264
                                                            CIP

This book is printed on paper suitable for recycling and made from fully managed and
sustained forest sources.

10   9   8   7   6   5   4   3   2   1
06   05   04   03   02   01   00   99   98   97

Printed in Hong Kong

Contents

A Note on References

References are cited throughout in brackets according to the numbering in the General Bibliography, with page and chapter references, where necessary, indicated by a colon after the bibliography number.

Acknowledgements

I am grateful to Richard Overy, the General Editor of this series, for suggesting that I should write this study and for his comments on the text, to Valery Rose of Longworth Editorial Services, and to Simon Winder of Macmillan. My thanks go as ever to my wife, Sue, and to my family for their encouragement and patience. Neil Hart, who taught me A-level history many years ago, kindly provided examples of recent examination questions. My thoughts on the subject owe much to the insights I have gained from teaching an MSc Special Subject at the London School of Economics on 'The Coming of War, 1911–14', and I am greatly indebted to the students who have taken it.

Editor's Preface

The main purpose of this series is to make available to teacher and student alike developments in a field of history that has become increasingly specialised with the sheer volume of new research and literature now produced. These studies are designed to present the 'state of the debate' on important themes and episodes in European history since the sixteenth century, presented in a clear and critical way by someone who is closely concerned himself with the debate.

The studies are not intended to be read as extended bibliographical essays, though each will contain a detailed guide to further reading which will lead students and the general reader quickly to key publications. Each book carries its own interpretation and conclusions, while locating the discussion firmly in the centre of the current issues as historians see them. It is intended that the series will introduce students to historical approaches which are in some cases very new and which, in the normal course of things, would take many years to filter down into the textbooks and school histories. I hope it will demonstrate some of the excitement historians, like scientists, feel as they work away in the vanguard of their subject.

The format of this series conforms closely with that of the companion series of studies in economic and social history which has already established a major reputation since its inception in 1968. Both series have an important contribution to make in publicising what it is that historians are doing and in making history more open and accessible. It is vital for history to communicate if it is to survive.

R. J. OVERY

Abbreviations

NB: see also the list of periodical abbreviations at the beginning of the Bibliography (p. 58).

BEF British Expeditionary Force
CGS Chief of the General Staff
CGT Confédération générale du travail (French trade-union federation)
ISB International Socialist Bureau
SFIO Section française de l'Internationale ouvrière (French socialist party)
SPD Sozialdemokratische Partei Deutschlands (German Social Democratic Party)

Chronology

1871   January: German Empire proclaimed.
      May: Frankfurt Peace Treaty; France cedes Alsace–Lorraine to Germany.
1878   July: Treaty of Berlin on Eastern Question.
1879   October: Dual Alliance (Germany, Austria–Hungary).
1881   June: Three Emperors' Alliance (Germany, Austria–Hungary, Russia).
1882   May: Triple Alliance (Germany, Austria–Hungary, Italy).
1887   June: Reinsurance Treaty (Germany, Russia).
1888   June: Wilhelm II becomes German Emperor.
1890   March: Bismarck resigns from German Chancellorship.
      June: Reinsurance Treaty expires.
1891   August: Franco-Russian political agreement.
1892   August: Franco-Russian military convention (ratified Dec. 1893–Jan. 1894).
1894   November: Nicholas II becomes Russian Emperor.
1897   May: Austro-Russian Balkan Agreement.
1898   March: German Naval Law.
      September–November: Fashoda Crisis (Britain and France).
1899   May–July: First Hague Peace Conference.
1899   October (to May 1902): South African War.
1900   June: German Naval Law.
1902   January: Anglo-Japanese alliance.
      November: Franco-Italian neutrality agreement (Prinetti–Barrère).
1903   June: Officers' coup in Serbia.
1904   February (to September 1905): Russo-Japanese War.
      April: Anglo-French colonial agreement (*Entente cordiale*).
1905   January: 'Bloody Sunday' massacre initiates revolutionary unrest in Russia.
      March: Tangier Incident opens First Moroccan Crisis.

1906 January: Anglo-French military discussions begin.
January–April: Algeciras Conference on Morocco.
February: HMS *Dreadnought* launched.
1907 June–October: Second Hague Peace Conference.
August: Anglo-Russian Entente.
1908 February: German Naval Law.
October: Austria–Hungary annexes Bosnia–Herzegovina.
1909 March: British naval estimates (four plus four dread-noughts). Secret agreement between German and Austro-Hungarian General Staffs. German ultimatum to Russia ends Bosnia annexation crisis.
June: Bethmann Hollweg replaces Bülow as German Chancellor.
1910 Russian army reorganisation.
November: Wilhelm II meets Nicholas II at Potsdam.
1911 July–November: Second Moroccan (Agadir) Crisis.
September (until October 1912): Italo-Turkish War.
1912 January: Poincaré becomes French Prime Minister.
February: Haldane Mission.
March: Serb–Bulgarian treaty begins formation of Balkan League (Serbia, Bulgaria, Greece, Montenegro).
June: German Navy and Army Laws.
July: Austro-Hungarian Army Law.
October: First Balkan War begins (Balkan League vs Turkey).
November: Adriatic port crisis. Anglo-French consultation agreement (Grey–Cambon letters).
December: Ambassadorial Conference opens in London. Potsdam 'War Council'.
1913 January: Poincaré elected French President.
April–May: Scutari Crisis.
May: London Treaty ends First Balkan War.
June–July: Second Balkan War (Bulgaria vs Serbia, Montenegro, Greece, Romania, Turkey).
July/August: Passage of German Army Law and French Three-Year Law.
August: Bucharest Treaty ends Second Balkan War.
October: Austro-Hungarian ultimatum to Serbia over Albanian frontier.
November (to January 1914): Liman von Sanders affair.

1914 January: Franco-Russian railway loan agreement.

March: German–Russian press war.

June: Anglo-Russian naval discussions.

28 June: Sarajevo assassinations.

5–6 July: German 'blank cheque' to Austria–Hungary.

7 July: Russian 'Great Programme' becomes law.

20–3 July: French state visit to Russia.

23 July: Austro-Hungarian ultimatum to Serbia.

25 July: Serbian reply and mobilisation. Austria–Hungary breaks off relations.

26 July: Russia begins pre-mobilisation measures. British conference proposal.

28 July: Austria–Hungary orders partial mobilisation and declares war on Serbia. Wilhelm II proposes halt in Belgrade.

29 July: Bombardment of Belgrade. German warnings to Russia and France. British warning to Germany. German neutrality bid. Nicholas II authorises partial mobilisation.

29–30 July: Bethmann Hollweg attempts to restrain Austria–Hungary.

30 July: French attempt to restrain Russia. Nicholas II authorises general mobilisation.

31 July: Russia begins general mobilisation. Germany declares state of danger of war and sends ultimata to Russia and France.

1 August: Germany declares war on Russia. French and German general mobilisations. Anglo-German 'misunderstanding'.

2 August: Germany invades Luxemburg and sends ultimatum to Belgium. British Cabinet decides to protect French coast and Belgian neutrality.

3 August: Germany invades Belgium and declares war on France. Italy proclaims neutrality.

4 August: Britain declares war on Germany.

6 August: Austria–Hungary declares war on Russia.

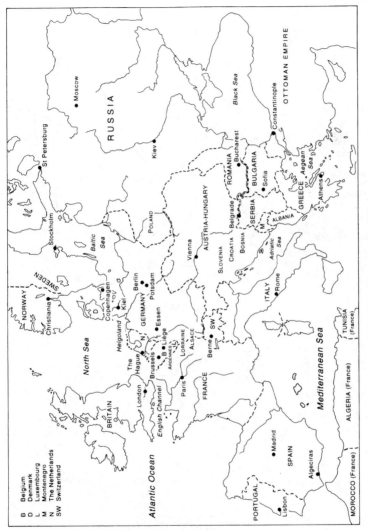

Map 1   Europe in 1914

B   Belgium
D   Denmark
L   Luxembourg
M   Montenegro
N   The Netherlands
SW   Switzerland

xiii

Map 2   The Balkans in 1914

Introduction

As this study was being written, images of Sarajevo flickered nightly across Western television screens, and commentators recalled that events there eighty years ago had started a world war. Although global politics in the 1990s have so far been less perilous than in the early twentieth century, with the break-up of the familiar framework provided by the Soviet–American Cold War they may not remain so. The most likely future is one of a return to a world of several competing Great Powers, manoeuvring in a hazardous environment of ethnic conflict, rivalry for markets and resources, and armaments races. If this happens, it will be more relevant than ever to examine why the pre-1914 Balkan tension so disastrously escalated.

What follows aims to introduce the student and the general reader to the vast historical literature on the origins of the First World War. It deliberately avoids a narrative account, which can easily be found elsewhere [9; 25; 27], although the principal events appear in the Chronology. The first four chapters focus on the July Crisis of 1914, examining the contribution made to it by each government, though setting the decision-making within a longer-term context. The fifth chapter is more general and interpretative. The Conclusion looks ahead to the decisions taken after the war broke out, which turned it into a long and devastating total conflict.

1 Austria–Hungary and Serbia

The First World War began over a local war, launched by the Dual Monarchy of Austria–Hungary against Serbia. The local war led almost instantaneously to a confrontation between the two blocs into which the six European Great Powers were divided (see Map 1). The Triple Alliance, dating from 1882, linked Austria–Hungary with Germany and Italy. The Triple Entente was based on the Franco-Russian Alliance, formed in 1891–4, with which Britain normally co-operated. Although Italy opted to stay neutral, Germany encouraged Austria–Hungary to attack Serbia, and was willing to risk and fight a general war rather than settle the issue peacefully. Russia was prepared to fight the Triple Alliance rather than see Serbia crushed; France to fight rather than repudiate its alliance with Russia; and Britain to fight rather than see France overwhelmed.

The Austro-Serb conflict was triggered by the murders of the Archduke Franz Ferdinand and his wife in Sarajevo, the capital of Bosnia, on 28 June 1914. Bosnia was part of Austria–Hungary, which was ruled by the Habsburg dynasty, and the Archduke was the heir to the throne. In an ultimatum on 23 July the government in Vienna accused Serbia of harbouring terrorist organisations that aimed to deprive the Habsburgs of Bosnia and their other territories inhabited by South Slavs. Serbian officials, it alleged, had helped organise the assassinations. Besides the punishment of those implicated, it demanded that anti-Habsburg publications and organisations should be suppressed, anti-Habsburg books and teachers eliminated from the schools, suspect officers and civil servants purged, and that Austrian representatives should take part in a judicial inquiry. The Serbian reply, on 25 July, unequivocally rejected only the last point, and accepted almost all even of the ultimatum's most extreme requirements [3: nos 37, 72]. None the less, Austria–Hungary at once broke off diplomatic relations, declared war on 28 July, and bombarded the Serbian capital, Belgrade, on the following day.

If the assassinations had not taken place, or if the ultimatum had been accepted unconditionally, there would have been no Austro-Serb war in the summer of 1914. We need to look at Serbia's responsibilities under these two heads. The Sarajevo conspirators – including Gavrilo Princip, who fired the fatal shots – were Bosnian Serbs and therefore Habsburg subjects. They belonged to a revolutionary movement, Young Bosnia, which indeed aimed to liberate Bosnia–Herzegovina, Croatia, and Slovenia from Austro-Hungarian rule (see Maps 1 and 2). It was true that Serbian officers and officials had given them bombs and revolvers in Belgrade and helped them cross the frontier. The problem was that the Serbian Government did not control its own intelligence services. Colonel Dimitrijević, or 'Apis', the military intelligence chief, was also leader of the Black Hand, an underground organisation dedicated to uniting all Serbs. He appears to have viewed Franz Ferdinand (mistakenly) as the head of the Austro-Hungarian war party, and hoped by removing him to hinder an attack. He had not consulted the Prime Minister, Nikola Pašić, and there was bitter enmity between the two men. When Pašić learned of the operation, he foresaw that it might provoke a war rather than prevent one, but it was difficult for him to repudiate it. He sent an ambiguous warning, which the Austrians failed to understand, and the security surrounding Franz Ferdinand's visit was lax [162; 163; 165].

Research into the tangled history of the assassinations has confirmed that the Serbian authorities must bear much of the blame. In addition, although Pašić and his Ministers toned down their reply on Russian advice, they were resolved to fight rather than completely submit, and if the Austrians insisted on a war they would be given one. But although both Apis and Pašić regarded an eventual showdown as inevitable, neither wanted it now. Serbia had only a tenth of Austria–Hungary's population. In the Balkan Wars of 1912–13 it had doubled its size, but for the moment its conquests were a liability that needed to be garrisoned against guerrilla resistance. Casualties had been heavy, there were shortages of shells and rifles, and the treasury was empty. Rejecting the ultimatum was a desperate gesture of defiance [28: ch. 3].

3

It was the Austrians rather than the Serbs who wished to force the issue. Because they knew a Balkan war was almost certain to expand into a wider conflict, it is extremely unlikely that they would have started one without the assurance on 5–6 July of German support, the so-called 'Potsdam blank cheque'. Once they had it, however, their Joint Council of Ministers agreed to impose 'such stringent demands ... that will make a refusal almost certain, so that the road to a radical solution by means of a military action should be opened' [3: no. 9]. To understand the Austrians' conduct we must consider both the Balkan and the European dimensions of their predicament, and how they came to harden their minds against moderation.

Under Ottoman Turkish rule for centuries, Bosnia and Herzegovina had been administered by Austria–Hungary since 1878, and annexed by it, causing an international crisis, in 1908, with the aim of blocking South Slav unification. In fact, the annexation intensified unrest. Young Bosnia and the Black Hand were formed in reaction, attacks began on Habsburg officials, and in 1913 the military governor suspended the Bosnian assembly. Violence was sporadic, however, and most of the population remained indifferent [164]. The South Slav problem caused such anxiety less because of the situation on the ground than because of the Dual Monarchy's peculiar internal make-up and the threat of outside intervention. Under the *Ausgleich*, or 'Compromise', of 1867, the two halves of the Monarchy shared a ruler – Franz Joseph was Austrian Emperor and King of Hungary – but had separate governments, parliaments, and budgets. The dominant nationalities (German-speakers in the Austrian half and Magyars in the Hungarian) accounted together for less than one in two of the total population. By 1914 conflict between Czechs and Germans had stalemated the Austrian legislature and the authorities ruled by decree. In Hungary the Magyars kept control only by discriminating against minorities such as the Croats and Romanians, who were increasingly alienated [64]. The drive for national self-determination seemed one of the dominating trends of modern European history, and it was natural to assume that a South Slav breakaway would set the dominoes tumbling.

Yet in 1914 there were still few demands for independence, and the army and civil service remained loyal. The real problem was that to domestic vulnerability was added the collapse of the

Habsburgs' Balkan predominance. A coup in 1903 had brought a new and more independent dynasty to the Serbian throne. The Serbs now sought loans and artillery from Paris rather than Vienna. When Austria–Hungary retaliated by boycotting their exports (chiefly livestock), in the 'pig war' of 1906–11, they found alternative markets. In the crisis of 1908–9 Vienna threatened invasion, forcing the Serbs to drop their objections to the annexation and to promise good behaviour, but Belgrade continued to encourage separatism. During the Balkan Wars of 1912–13 there were further clashes, the Austrians insisting on the creation of a new state of Albania to limit Serbia's gains. This failed to compensate for the virtual expulsion from Europe of Turkey, which had previously served as a counterbalance, especially as in 1913–14 Romania, which had secretly been allied to Austria–Hungary and Germany since 1883, abandoned the alliance in all but name and became another potential enemy [61; 71].

The danger was made acute by the Dual Monarchy's isolation among the Great Powers. For a decade after an agreement made in 1897 Vienna and St Petersburg had co-operated in maintaining the Balkan status quo, but relations never recovered from the Bosnian crisis, during which Austria–Hungary and Germany browbeat the Russians into abandoning the Serbs. In the run-up to 1914 the Austrians faced a Russian build-up on their northeastern frontier and the possibility that a new Balkan League, similar to that established against Turkey with Russian backing in 1912, would be created against them. But after the formation of the Triple Entente France and Britain were unlikely to back Austria–Hungary against Russia, and Italy, supposedly an ally, was unreliable. Italy had been unified in the nineteenth century at Austria's expense, and there were still Italians under Habsburg rule. Rome and Vienna jockeyed for advantage in the Balkans, and were competitors in an Adriatic naval race. Finally, even from Germany there was no consistent diplomatic support [62; 71].

Austrian leaders preferred to settle crises peacefully, but the belief was growing that force was unavoidable. Economic pressure against Serbia was counterproductive, and promises of good behaviour were worthless. General Franz Conrad von Hötzendorf, who as Chief of the General Staff (CGS) was responsible for war planning, was the longest-standing advocate of a military solution, and experience in the Balkan Wars seemed to vindicate him. The

Foreign Minister, Count Berchtold, tried at first to coordinate with the other Powers his response to the upheaval. He became disillusioned, and in crises with Serbia's ally, Montenegro, over Scutari in April–May 1913 and with Serbia itself over the Albanian eastern frontier in October, he found that unilateral threats were a better means of getting his way. But calling out extra troops to support his demands was extremely expensive and demoralised the conscripts. Conrad argued that a short, sharp war would be preferable to endless alerts. By the autumn of 1913 Berchtold probably agreed with him, but there was no advance decision to provoke a conflict and in June 1914 the Foreign Ministry was looking for German co-operation in a new diplomatic offensive [61; 63; 66; 71].

It was therefore Sarajevo and the blank cheque that made military action the immediate preference. Franz Ferdinand's death eliminated the man who had been Conrad's most consistent critic. It removed most of Berchtold's and Franz Joseph's remaining reservations about going to war, and supplied a convenient pretext. The Hungarian Premier, István Tisza, however, still opposed using force, and even Conrad recognised that in view of the risk of Russian involvement there must be German backing. A pro-war consensus had not been completely established when the head of Berchtold's personal office at the Foreign Ministry, the hawkish diplomat Count Hoyos, was sent on the crucial mission to Germany with letters from his chief and from Franz Joseph that strongly hinted at war against Serbia without explicitly advocating it. But Germany's emphatic response settled the matter for most of the Monarchy's leaders, even though Tisza held out until mid-July. He was won over partly by the fear that unless Austria–Hungary acted it would never receive such support again. He was assured that Romania would not attack and that Serbian territory would be assigned to Albania and Bulgaria in order to minimise the additional Slav population brought into the Monarchy. From now on the Austro-Hungarian authorities barely hesitated in their drive towards hostilities [65; 68; 69].

Their decision originated from the developing confrontation with the South Slavs over the previous decade and the shift in the Balkan balance against Vienna since 1912, as well as in underlying fears about international isolation and internal decay. But the assassinations themselves were indispensable as a catalyst. There were grounds for saying that the circumstances were favourable, given that Serbia and Montenegro were exhausted and Italy and Romania likely at least not to oppose the Monarchy and possibly even to side with it. Conrad had been told that the German General Staff was confident of victory over France, and he expected (wrongly) a German supporting offensive against Russia [67]. At Tisza's insistence, moreover, the Habsburg leaders had worked out in advance what they would do with a Balkan victory. Yet the conclusion is inescapable that there was a fatalistic irresponsibility in their decision-making, and the near certainty of war with Russia was accepted without proper consideration of the alternatives or the implications being thought through. After years of provocation, patience snapped [70: ch. 3].

2 Germany and the Blank Cheque

Far from being a stooge of its stronger ally, Austria–Hungary was an independent Power whose initiative was indispensable. None the less, a German veto would probably have halted it in its tracks, steering it back towards less draconian demands that Serbia and Russia could swallow. But when Hoyos arrived at Potsdam on 5 July, the Emperor Wilhelm II advised him, as reported by the Austro-Hungarian Ambassador, that Vienna should take 'warlike action' and 'march into Serbia'. Russia was unprepared and would 'think twice' about fighting, but if it did intervene 'Germany, our old faithful ally, would stand at our side'. On 6 July Wilhelm's Chancellor (the head of his government), Theobald von Bethmann Hollweg, confirmed that Germany recommended 'immediate action' against Serbia, and that 'whatever way we decide, we may always be certain that we will find Germany at our side' [3: nos 6, 8].

For most of the crisis the Germans stuck to this line. Knowing in advance the substance of the ultimatum, they pressed the Austrians to deliver it without delay, and then for an early declaration of war. British mediation proposals were forwarded to Vienna with advice not to co-operate [3: nos 95, 96]. Only on 29–30 July was there a short-lived effort by Bethmann to hold Austria–Hungary back. By this stage Russia's military preparations were becoming alarming, and warnings were delivered to St Petersburg and Paris. But the Russians mobilised their forces regardless, and on 31 July Germany issued an ultimatum to them to desist, with one to France requiring its neutrality in a Russo-German conflict. As neither demand was accepted, Berlin declared war on Russia and France on 1 and 3 August respectively, setting in motion its war plan, the Schlieffen–Moltke Plan, which envisaged invading Belgium and Luxemburg in order to outflank French defences. After the Germans sent an ultimatum to Belgium to allow the passage of troops and ignored a British ultimatum to respect the country's independence, on 4 August Britain, too, entered the war.

The German Government unquestionably desired and encouraged an Austro-Serb conflict. In the end it initiated war against Russia and France, although alleging that Russian mobilisation had provoked it. Finally, rather than modify its plan of campaign, it reluctantly accepted hostilities with Britain, opening a conflict that spread far beyond Europe's shores. These distinctions between the local, Continental, and global stages of escalation must be kept in mind when approaching the problem of responsibility. In the notorious 'war-guilt clause', Article 231 of the 1919 Treaty of Versailles, the victorious Powers justified their claim for reparations by asserting that the world war had been 'imposed upon them by the aggression of Germany and her allies'. As the struggle over reparations poisoned international politics for the next decade, the war-guilt controversy was not only intensely emotive but acutely topical. During the 1920s the German Foreign Ministry orchestrated a counter-offensive, subsidising books and journals that set out the 'revisionist' or anti-Versailles case, and a tradition of 'patriotic self-censorship' led most German historians to co-operate [17; 50: pp. 262–301; 126]. More extreme revisionists alleged that Germany had simply been defending itself against aggressive encirclement by the Triple Entente; more moderate ones that all the Powers had been victims of the international system. In the widely cited words of the wartime British Prime Minister, David Lloyd George, 'The nations slithered over the brink into the boiling cauldron of war' [85: vol. 1, p. 52].

Even after the Second World War, revisionism was widely accepted within Germany and to some extent outside, a committee of French and German historians agreeing in 1951 that 'the documents do not permit attributing [sic] a premeditated desire for a European war on the part of any government or people in 1914' [19: p. 64]. 1939 could be blamed on the Nazis, whom the leading German historians represented as a bizarre, aberrant phenomenon, out of keeping with national traditions. But if Germany had been the aggressor in 1914 as well, it would seem to be a permanent danger to European peace, and should be kept divided indefinitely. These considerations help explain the ferocious reaction when revisionism was challenged by Professor Fritz Fischer, and in response to that reaction the 'Fischer thesis' itself became more radical [17; 107; 126; 132].

Fischer's first major study was later translated into English as *Germany's Aims in the First World War*, but its original title of *Griff nach der Weltmacht* ('Grasp for World Power') better conveys its flavour. The German edition appeared in 1961, the year of the building of the Berlin wall [115]. Its theme was less the origins of the 1914–18 war than Germany's 'war aims' during it, and its most striking revelation was the 'September Programme' of aims approved by Bethmann Hollweg on 9 September 1914. This and other documents showed that Germany had wanted a chain of buffer states (including Belgium in the west and Russia's Polish and Baltic provinces in the east) under its economic and military control. It had also sought a worldwide system of naval bases, a colonial empire in Central Africa, and a customs union (known as *Mitteleuropa*) embracing Central and Western Europe. The objective was permanent security in west and east and a comparable territorial base to those of the emerging 'World Powers' of the British Empire, Russia, and the USA, with whom the future was thought to lie.

Two aspects of Fischer's portrayal were especially controversial. First, he believed that there was an expansionist consensus among the German elites, and that victory abroad was intended to consolidate the established order at home. He assumed the 'primacy of domestic policy' or *Primat der Innenpolitik*: that foreign policy was principally determined by internal political goals. This challenged the prevailing assumption in German historical writing of the 'primacy of external policy' or *Primat der Aussenpolitik*: that foreign policy was principally determined by factors such as geography and the balance of power, and the highest purpose of the state was to pursue external objectives [107]. Characteristic was Fischer's tendency to minimise the differences between the civilian leaders, such as Bethmann, and the military chiefs. It brought him into conflict with the senior historian of the previous generation, Gerhard Ritter, who had stressed the military's dangerous independence and irresponsibility [135; 136]. Fischer may have overstated his case, but he made it impossible to continue viewing Bethmann as a well-meaning 'good German' who did his best to avoid war.

More provocative still was Fischer's assertion of the continuity of German history. As well as hinting at parallels between Germany's ambitions in the First World War and in the Second, he drew parallels between the 1914–18 war aims and *Weltpolitik*, or 'world policy', the new course taken by Berlin's foreign policy in the 1890s. He showed that publicists and officials had already been interested in *Mitteleuropa* and Central Africa before war broke out, with the implication that 1914 was a case of premeditated aggression rather than a defensive response to encirclement [16, 2nd edn: ch. 5; 116]. Yet his initial assessment of the July Crisis itself, while firmly anti-revisionist, was measured. All the Powers bore blame, but 'as Germany willed and coveted the Austro-Serbian war and, in her confidence in her military superiority, deliberately faced the risk of a conflict with Russia and France, her leaders must bear a substantial share of the historical responsibility for the outbreak of general war' [115: p. 86].

Fischer's *War of Illusions*, in contrast, appearing in German in 1969 and in English translation in 1975, alleged that Sarajevo was seized on as a pretext to launch a pre-planned Continental offensive [117: pp. 470, 515]. It assigned a pivotal position to the Potsdam 'War Council' of 8 December 1912, convened by Wilhelm at a moment in the First Balkan War that prefigured the circumstances of July 1914. Serbian troops had driven through Turkish territory to the Adriatic, defying Austrian objections to a Serbian sea outlet. Bethmann had announced that if Austria–Hungary imposed its will and Russia intervened, Berlin would support Vienna. The British then warned that if fighting spread to Western Europe they would assist France, and Wilhelm, incensed, called at Potsdam for immediate war against the Triple Entente. The Chief of the General Staff (CGS), Helmuth von Moltke the younger, agreed, but the Navy Secretary, Alfred von Tirpitz, said he needed another eighteen months. The idea of fighting now was dropped – and in fact Serbia had already decided to give way [137; 138].

Fischer, however, portrayed the War Council as deciding not to reject European war but to defer it, and to prepare the country in the meantime. As evidence he cited the massive army bill of 1913, attempts to ready public opinion, financial precautions, and efforts to win Balkan allies and secure British neutrality. He documented the breakthrough of a radical Right that called for a more aggressive and authoritarian regime. The Reich was headed into a *cul-de-sac*, checked by the Triple Entente abroad and beset by rising opposition at home. Increasingly, thoughts turned to violence, domination of the Continent being the precondition for renewed expansion worldwide [117: chs 9–19].

The 'Fischer controversy' overturned the orthodoxy of the 1950s without any one view replacing it, and Fischer has rightly claimed that it helped democratise not only the historical profession but German society generally [119]. The interpretation of the July Crisis in his first book, however, has won much wider acceptance than that in his second. We must now examine more closely the domestic and external influences on German policy, before reconsidering the origins of the blank cheque.

Professor Arno Mayer has highlighted the persistence of the pre-French Revolution ancien régime ('old regime') in the social structures and modes of thought of early twentieth-century Europe [34]. The founding statesman of the German Empire, Otto von Bismarck, had tried to base autocracy on consent. The lower chamber of parliament, the Reichstag, was elected by adult male suffrage, and its approval was needed for legislation and budgets. But it lacked the power to initiate either, or to hold ministers responsible. Wilhelm appointed and dismissed the Chancellor, and could run foreign policy with little consultation. In addition, Bismarck had set precedents for using foreign successes as a means of capturing domestic support. Since Fischer a number of historians have seen 1914 as another such 'flight forward' (*Flucht nach vorn*) out of a domestic impasse [144].

This view has rightly been criticised. Volker Berghahn has pointed out that there is no *a priori* reason to give precedence to internal or external factors in explaining foreign policy: both contribute, although the balance between them varies. At the turn of the century internal factors were arguably uppermost. France and Russia were at loggerheads with Britain, and Germany was not much threatened abroad. *Weltpolitik*, the brainchild of Wilhelm II and a new generation of advisers, sought to assert Berlin's influence globally. It was supported by the Navy Laws of 1898 and 1900, designed to create a powerful battlefleet. The aim was to put pressure on Britain and win commercial opportunities and territory, but also to smooth out the business cycle through naval building and to unite the monarchy's supporters [105; 129].

Weltpolitik failed spectacularly on almost every count, and by the last years before 1914 Germany's international position had greatly deteriorated. The authorities' internal difficulties had also worsened, but not so seriously, and certainly less than in Austria–Hungary where domestic pressures alone caused the drift to war. After Britain launched HMS *Dreadnought* in 1906 and a new era opened of all-big-gun battleships, the German naval budget far exceeded expectations, and arguments over financing it divided the pro-government parties [105; 120]. The opposition Social Democratic Party, or SPD, became the largest grouping in the Reichstag in 1912. Despite its rhetoric, it was not a revolutionary organisation, but it did want greater democracy and in 1913–14 was debating using mass strikes in order to get it [108]. On the other hand, the extreme nationalism of the Pan-German League was infecting the more mainstream right-wing parties, which were now attacking Wilhelm in person. Yet Bethmann was distrustful of the Right and discouraged talk of *coups d'état* and preventive war. The latter, he told the Bavarian representative in Berlin in June 1914, would benefit socialism and might 'topple a few thrones' [123: p. 171]. There is little evidence that domestic calculations prompted the blank cheque.

On the other hand, testimony is abundant that the external situation was causing grave concern. Its outstanding features were diplomatic isolation and an arms race, against a backdrop of mounting tension. In 1902 Italy secretly agreed with France to stay neutral in a war between the two alliances, possibly even if France started the fighting. Britain made ententes, or spheres-of-influence agreements, with France in 1904 and Russia in 1907, alleviating the three Powers' extra-European differences. In the Moroccan Crisis of 1905–6 the German Government hoped that it could profit from Russia's defeats in the Far East in order to weaken both the Anglo-French Entente and the Franco-Russian Alliance by obstructing France's efforts to gain control of Morocco. But Britain gave France diplomatic support and agreed to secret staff talks, and in the Bosnian Crisis it co-operated with Russia. By the time Bethmann became Chancellor in 1909 the German leaders were openly complaining of 'encirclement', and he considered that 'to split up the coalition directed against us' was his highest priority in foreign policy [117: p. 63].

At the Potsdam summit meeting in 1910 Bethmann tried to improve relations with Russia by agreeing on spheres of influence in Asia, but the détente broke down after the first Balkan War. In the winter of 1913–14 the two Powers clashed when Germany strengthened its military mission in Turkey, General Liman von Sanders being designated to command the Ottoman army corps stationed at the Dardanelles. The Russians regarded the Turkish Straits as a vital artery, through which they sent nearly half their exports, and although a compromise was reached relations remained strained [149: ch. 4; 150]. In discussions with Britain, meanwhile, in 1909–12, Bethmann offered to slow down the naval expansion in exchange for a pledge of neutrality in a Continental conflict, which London refused. Anglo-German relations improved in 1912–14, but after the von Sanders affair the Russians wanted more support from Britain, which agreed to secret naval discussions. The news was leaked to the German Embassy, but when questioned in the House of Commons in June 1914 the Foreign Secretary, Sir Edward Grey, appeared to deny the talks' existence, thus undermining Berlin's confidence in his good faith. Bethmann's efforts to break out of encirclement by diplomacy were making little headway.

Still more ominous was the emergence of an inter-bloc arms race. During the first decade of the century the pace of change in the big four Continental armies – in Germany, Austria–Hungary, Russia and France – was slow. The Anglo-German naval rivalry was the most dynamic in Europe. Tirpitz's 1908 Navy Law raised the German construction tempo to four new dreadnought battleships or battlecruisers each year. In 1909–10 Britain retaliated by laying down eight, and from then on kept consistently ahead. Meanwhile, however, the Russian army was being reorganised in 1910, accelerating its mobilisation, and under the impact of the Second Moroccan, or Agadir, Crisis in 1911 the French army speeded up reform and the Germans correctly judged it to be more willing to fight. In the *Rüstungswende*, or 'armaments turning-point', of 1912, Berlin reorientated its priorities. Naval construction dropped back to two new dreadnoughts annually, while the army was notably expanded. The Austrians also passed an army bill, and rivalry on land between the two alliances now dominated the scene [52].

The Balkan Wars intensified this trend. Their outcome meant that in any future European conflict Austria–Hungary would be obliged to send additional forces southwards and, therefore, could give less help to Germany against Russia. Germany's 1913 army law was intended to compensate. Previously the Berlin War Ministry had objected that expansion would mean recruiting more middle-class (rather than aristocratic) officers and more working-class (rather than peasant) soldiers. That such arguments were set aside shows how the German leaders were now more worried about the military balance than about democratisation [120]. Furthermore, the law was financed by a capital levy that was opposed by the Conservatives but supported by the SPD, which had voted against the army bill itself. There was no shortage of wealth in Germany, but the authorities were nearing the limits to rearmament because of disagreements over how to pay for it [113; 114]. Yet, meanwhile France had responded to Germany's law by passing one to extend its own military service from two years to three. In January 1914 it agreed with Russia on a 2500 million franc loan, in return for which the Russians would build over 5000 kilometres of strategic railways by 1918, further accelerating their deployment. Finally, in July the Russian Parliament approved the 'Great Programme', which would enlarge the tsarist standing army by 40 per cent over three years. And, unlike Germany, Russia was feeling little financial strain [101; 151; 152].

The German war plan, the brainchild of Alfred von Schlieffen, CGS in 1890–1905, and subsequently modified by Moltke, assumed that a European war would be fought on two fronts. Plans for a first offensive to the east were shelved in 1913, it being thought that the best chance of victory was to overwhelm the French before the more slowly gathering Russians could threaten Berlin [134]. But Russia's 1910 reorganisation and the projected railway improvements, as well as the diversion of Austrian forces to the Balkans, would magnify the dangers entailed in leaving the eastern frontier exposed. The Germans barely outnumbered even the French army, and in 1913 a law was passed to reinforce the Belgian one, threatening Moltke's hopes of sweeping through Belgium after capturing the crucial railway junction at Liège within the first seventy-two hours. Berlin seemed outmatched in the arms race and destined to lose it, but in 1914 a last chance

presented itself. Germany's 1913 law had largely been implemented, whereas its opponents' measures would take full effect
only from 1917. The Three-Year Law may temporarily even have
damaged the French army, because it entailed calling up a higher
proportion of untrained recruits. In May or June Moltke told the
Foreign Minister, Gottlieb von Jagow, that victory was still possible
but in three years would not be, and Germany's leaders should
seek an opportunity to start a preventive war. This does not mean
that the authorities in July 1914 were necessarily acting as Moltke
suggested, but when they entered the Sarajevo Crisis they had
been extensively briefed on the strategic trends [52; 117].

Moltke's recommendation assumed that Germany could not
simply sit back and let the Triple Entente gain the advantage.
Unfortunately the final element in the international situation was
a general increase in tension and a sense of heightened danger.
The principal reason, apart from armaments, was the succession of
diplomatic crises, over Morocco in 1905–6 and 1911, the Balkans
in 1908–9 and 1912–13, and the Turkish Straits in 1913–14. Agadir
set off a chain reaction, prompting Italy to go to war with Turkey
in 1911 in order to seize Libya, and then the Balkan League to
attack the Turks in 1912. Either a scramble for the Ottoman
Empire in Asia or a further Balkan flare-up loomed. Further confrontations were likely, while Bethmann's diplomacy was failing
and the armaments ratio moving further against Berlin.

This does not mean that a premeditated decision was taken at
any time before Sarajevo to force a war. Fischer himself no longer
maintains that the War Council decided to start a conflict in eighteen months' time [119], and Professor John Röhl has suggested
that if there was such a decision it came in the spring or early
summer of 1914 [28: ch. 2]. The archival documentation (which,
admittedly, is incomplete) shows no line of continuous preparation from December 1912. The 1913 army bill had been agreed in
principle before the War Council met, and even afterwards was
not expanded by as much as Moltke wanted. The bill can be ade-
quately explained as a response to the Balkan Crisis and a precaution against a possible European war, rather than proving an
intention to start one. It is true that Tirpitz asked at the Council
for time to complete the defences of the island of Helgoland and
the widening of the Kiel Canal (so as to allow dreadnoughts to
pass between the North and Baltic Seas) and that the work was

finished in June 1914. But the Navy Staff regarded Germany's numerical inferiority in warships as more important than the Canal, and although a new construction bill was prepared after the War Council it was quickly abandoned. There is no evidence that the authorities were consistently working up public opinion after December 1912 and, on the contrary, there is some evidence that Bethmann tried to dampen down war fever [52; 117: pp. 190–8, 268–70].

It is necessary to understand how the Berlin bureaucracy operated. Responsibility for co-ordination lay with Wilhelm, to whom the military and naval chiefs had direct access without going via the civilian ministers. But the Emperor was an erratic and inconsistent posturer, who was unequal to his task. It would be naïve to treat his outbursts at face value. Characteristically the War Council included neither Bethmann nor the Foreign Minister, and not even the War Minister, who were all informed about it afterwards. Agencies such as the Navy Office and the General Staff were capable of long-range planning, but it is questionable if this was possible for the government as a whole [125].

All the same, it is obviously significant that the controllers of the most formidable army in Europe were debating whether or not to unleash it, and despite Bethmann's absence from the War Council Wilhelm reported soon afterwards that the Chancellor was no longer opposed in principle to hostilities [137: p. 665]. From December 1912, if not from even earlier, force was moving to the forefront among the options under consideration, and by the spring of 1914 it was more prominent still, due mainly to anxiety about tsarist intentions. In March there was a press war, German newspapers warning of the danger when St Petersburg was ready in two to three years' time, and Russian ones replying that their country would not be intimidated into abandoning its build-up. Moltke kept Wilhelm and Bethmann fully briefed on military developments. Yet up until July plans were still under discussion for a programme of strategic railway building and a possible army reinforcement in 1916 (though the money was lacking), which would make no sense if there was already a commitment to an early strike [52; 141].

We may now return to the blank cheque. It was decided on in a series of dispersed meetings when many prominent figures were away on vacation. Wolfgang Mommsen has suggested that it resulted from a sudden convergence of views between leaders with differing expectations and agendas [130]. Wilhelm started the ball rolling by giving Hoyos his backing on 5 July, moved apparently by sentiments of outrage and of monarchical solidarity, although in the previous October he had already encouraged Conrad to attack the Serbs. He said that he expected hostilities to remain localised but that if Russia mobilised he would fight [3: no. 6]. He repeated the last point to the armaments manufacturer, Krupp von Bohlen und Halbach, on the same day [117: p. 478]. Moltke's recent conversation with Jagow may mean that the General Staff Chief, in contrast, would have wanted escalation, although he was among those who were out of town and not involved in the deliberations. The most inscrutable case is that of Bethmann, who with Jagow was responsible for handling the crisis while Wilhelm departed from 6 to 28 July on a Baltic cruise. The Chancellor's papers were destroyed in the Second World War, but during the Fischer controversy extracts were published from the diaries of his assistant, Kurt Riezler [109; 124; 127–8; 133]. They suggested that Bethmann consciously risked a European bloodbath, because of fear of losing Austria–Hungary, exasperation over the Anglo-Russian naval talks, and, above all, foreboding about Russia. He was willing either for a Balkan blitzkrieg that might break up the Triple Entente, or for Continental war while the prospects still seemed favourable. More recently it has become clear that the July 1914 entries are in a different format from the rest of Riezler's manuscript, and almost certainly were rewritten after the event. Yet the picture given in them is partially corroborated in other parts of the diaries themselves as well as by documents of uncontested authenticity drafted in the Chancellery or the Foreign Ministry at the time [106; 109; 140]. In both agencies it was agreed that the chances of containing the crisis depended largely on what Russia would do. Taken together, the evidence suggests that the German leaders (probably apart from Moltke) preferred and worked for a localised Austro-Serb conflict: which supports Fischer's earlier rather than his later position. Fischer is right to argue (see Chapter 4 below) that Bethmann wished to avoid hostilities with Britain, but both Wilhelm and his Chancellor were willing to start a conflict with Russia and France rather than back down. It is at best a half truth to say that they did not 'want' war.

The immediate reason for issuing the blank cheque was to back Vienna. There was no need to give it under the terms of the Austro-German Alliance of 1879 or the Triple Alliance of 1882, both of which were defensive. Although in 1909 and 1912 the Germans had promised to assist if Austria–Hungary were attacked by Russia while using force against Serbia [67; 71], in the spring and summer of 1913 they had discouraged hasty action. But since then they had apparently come to fear that their ally might abandon them or even disintegrate unless they supported it more strongly [73: pp. 111, 117]. The two camps were sufficiently equal for the Balkan balance of power to be crucial to that in Europe generally, and apart from the bond between the ruling dynasties and a shared Germanic culture, the Habsburg army was essential to German strategy. If the Dual Monarchy broke up, its German-speakers might have to be absorbed into Germany, which would strengthen Catholic and decentralising tendencies against the Protestant Hohenzollern dynasty. These considerations, as well as hatred of subversion, were enough to justify supporting a localised war, and the blank cheque was easier to give because it seemed possible that Vienna would not cash it. But if it did, a localised conflict would humiliate Russia and perhaps destroy the Triple Entente; and in a Continental one at least Germany would fight in the certainty that Austria–Hungary was at its side. Although this interpretation stresses (with Fischer's critics) the opportunist and defensive character of German policy, the Berlin leaders had still embarked upon an extraordinarily dangerous course, and only general European considerations, as well as Balkan developments, can explain their willingness to do so. Whether a decision to risk a Continental conflagration would become a decision to start one now depended on their potential enemies.

3 Russo-French Response

The Austro-German challenge confronted the powers of the Triple Entente with the alternatives of letting Serbia be overwhelmed or preparing for a European war. Although they searched for a middle road, they quickly realised that they must choose between the two evils and they opted for the latter. The decision was first and foremost one for Russia, where the Council of Ministers on 24 July and a Crown Council (chaired by Tsar Nicholas II) on the following day agreed not to abandon Belgrade. Diplomatic avenues would be explored, but premobilisation preparations would begin on 26 July against both Austria–Hungary and Germany, and, if necessary, Russia would undertake a partial mobilisation against the Dual Monarchy. Once it became clear that the two Central Powers meant business there was a second period of debate, at the end of which Nicholas ordered partial mobilisation on 29 July and altered this on the 30th to general mobilisation against both Berlin and Vienna, Day One being the 31st. The reply was Germany's ultimatum.

Once again the regional considerations must be disentangled from the broader ones. Russia was the Power with the biggest and longest standing interest in what had come to be known as the 'Eastern Question': that of what would happen if the decay of the Ottoman Turkish Empire in Europe and Asia turned into a collapse. During the nineteenth century alone there had been Russo-Turkish wars in 1806–12, 1828–9, 1853–6, and 1877–8, and the other Powers were all more or less anxious that Turkish decline and the consequent expansion of Russia and its Balkan protégés would add dangerously to tsarist strength. Conversely, the need to counterbalance German backing for Austria–Hungary in the region had been a major reason for Russia's entry into the alliance with France. As 1914 approached, the Turkish decline seemed to be accelerating, the wars with Italy and the Balkan League intensified the pressure, and deepening antagonism between Austria–Hungary and the South Slavs in the Balkans and between Berlin and St Petersburg at the Dardanelles featured among the consequences. None the less, on the eve of war neither the Russians nor any of the other Powers believed it in their interest to see what was left of the Turkish Empire being partitioned between them [149; 153].

In addition, although Russian governments and public opinion had for decades viewed the Eastern Question as being of central importance, their stakes in it if considered objectively were arguably too small to justify such concern. Russia's markets and investments in Serbia itself were minimal, although it is true that the Balkans were seen as a protective screen between the Central Powers and the Turkish Straits, where tsarist economic interests were much more significant. Militarily, on the other hand, Serbia and Montenegro, especially if combined with Romania, could greatly assist Russia against Austria–Hungary. However, as Barbara Jelavich has rightly argued, the Russians' commitment cannot be reduced to such cold-blooded calculations. They shared with Serbia Orthodox Christianity and a Slavonic language. There was a tradition of assisting the Balkan Slavs, and the Pan-Slav movement claimed that Russia had a 'historic mission' to do so, to which the government paid lip service [149: ch. 4; 154]. Yet there was no treaty obligation, and over Bosnia in 1909 and Albania in 1912–13 Nicholas had advised Serbia and Montenegro to give way. What made the difference this time?

Part of the answer is that the challenge was much more radical. Previously Serbia's independence had not been threatened, but now, although the Austrians offered not to annex territory, they appeared determined to overrun the country and reluctant to negotiate. The Russian Foreign Minister, Sergei Sazonov, told his colleagues on 24 July that the aim was to make Serbia a *de facto* protectorate, and if they acquiesced their Balkan influence would 'collapse utterly'. But in addition the Ministers agreed that behind Vienna stood Berlin, and that past moderation had encouraged German aggression. Peace would best be protected by firmness, but if firmness failed Russia must 'make the sacrifices required of her' [155].

There had been a gradual breakdown in the conservative alliance between the (Russian) Romanov and (Prusso-German)

Hohenzollern dynasties. The rise of Pan-Slavism and of German racist nationalism were partly to blame. Since the 1880s the German authorities had obstructed loans to the Russian Government (which instead came mainly from France), and the 1904 trade treaty between the two countries, which the Russians thought unfavourable, was coming up for renewal. To the friction caused by Germany's support for Austria–Hungary was added the new flashpoint at the Dardanelles, and not only did the Russians remain loyal to the French alliance but they hoped to reinforce their ties with Paris and London. As the arms race gathered momentum both the von Sanders episode and the press war strengthened their determination not to be bullied [12: ch. 4; 153].

The Russians felt that they must act, not simply protest, and it was they who began the militarisation of the July Crisis. Yet all the Powers understood that military precautions could be misinterpreted as signalling an intention to fight. In November 1912, for example, during the First Balkan War, Sazonov and the then Prime Minister, Kokovtsov, had been horrified when Nicholas consented to a partial mobilisation of the Kiev military district, and had got the measure annulled as being too provocative [27; 49: ch. 1]. Even after the delivery of the ultimatum in 1914 Germany and Austria–Hungary did little to raise their preparedness, hoping this would assist them to contain the conflict. Unfortunately Kokovtsov had now been replaced by an elderly non-entity, Goremykin, and Sazonov was increasingly inclined to armed diplomacy, having considered occupying Turkish territory during the von Sanders affair. He had already been contemplating mobilisation before the ultimatum arrived.

The terminology needs clarification. The standing armies of the Continental Powers were composed of professional career soldiers and of conscripts doing military service (which normally lasted two or three years). Reservists were conscripts who had completed their service but were still liable for call-up. Mobilisation meant adding the reservists and bringing the units up to war strength before transporting them to the frontiers, an operation known as concentration. For Russia, as for every other Power except Germany, neither mobilisation nor concentration were synonymous with war, as the soldiers could still be halted on the borders. The aim of threatening partial mobilisation was to make Vienna back down. On the other hand, the pre-mobilisation measures implemented against both Central Powers from 26 July included cancelling leave, pre-positioning railway wagons, and purchasing horses. If war resulted they would therefore speed up concentration not only against Austria–Hungary but also against Germany, and they set a clock ticking under the Schlieffen–Moltke Plan [26; 47: ch. 11].

The Russian measures dramatically accelerated the tempo of the crisis and wrecked their antagonists' localisation strategy. German military intelligence soon detected them [141], and on 29 July Bethmann warned that if they continued Germany would have to mobilise and European war could 'scarcely' be prevented: on the same day news came of the bombardment of Belgrade. These developments persuaded Sazonov that general war was 'inevitable', and there was no choice but to order general mobilisation. Nicholas still preferred the half-measure of a partial call-up, but on the afternoon of 30 July Sazonov won him round. Neither had illusions about what they were doing, Nicholas saying that general mobilisation meant sending 'thousands and thousands of men to their deaths' [3: nos 127, 136–7, 147; 53: p. 80].

Yet during the von Sanders affair the tsarist leaders had discussed war with Germany and agreed that it was not at that time desirable. The General Staff wanted calm, to press on with re-armament, and the Russians' advantage, unlike Germany's, was to wait [52]. There are arguments for saying that they fought because of misleading advice. Sazonov saw partial mobilisation as a middle road, that might sway Vienna without provoking Berlin. Jagow led him on by suggesting on the 27th that Germany could tolerate a partial mobilisation, before reversing his position on 29 July [3: nos 103, 110, 138]. Janushkevich, the new and inexperienced Chief of the General Staff, at first failed to warn that railway schedules had not been prepared for a partial call-up, which if implemented would have left Russia dangerously exposed against Germany. Later on, he joined the rest of the military in insisting on a general measure. However, it is doubtful whether a middle road ever existed. Bethmann's warning on 29 July suggests that even a continuation of the pre-mobilisation measures would have driven Germany into war. If the Austrians were determined to invade Serbia, Russia's only real choice was whether or not to resist by force. From the beginning the Council of Ministers was willing to do so if necessary, and by the time that Sazonov pressed for general mobilisation he had decided that European war was unavoidable [47: ch. 11; 155].

Two factors helped the Russians to take the plunge. First, it seems that they expected their home front to hold. This was in spite of the revolutionary movement that had followed defeat by Japan, and a recent upsurge of working-class unrest, culminating in July 1914 in a general strike in St Petersburg. The press supported Serbia, and the Interior Ministry advised that the peasants would obey the call-up. Sazonov warned Nicholas that *unless* he assisted Belgrade he risked 'revolution and the loss of his throne' [12: ch. 4; 33; 157: p. 109].

Second, although the War and Navy Ministers reported that their forces were unprepared, they agreed that firmness was the best course. War was no longer inconceivable, as it had been at the time of the Bosnian Crisis. The Russians knew that they were stronger than the Austrians, and expected France to take Germany's first blow. The French military were optimistic, and the French civilians affirmed that Russia could count on them [51; 52].

This leads into the influence of Russia's partners. Sazonov believed that the British Navy was the best deterrent against Germany, but he failed to get an early promise of London's support. This made it the more imperative to win French backing. If Paris had held Russia back (as it did in 1909) it is unlikely that St Petersburg would have acted alone, although its resentment might have destroyed the alliance. In fact, as will be seen, partly because the French Government was temporarily leaderless, the Russians received their own version of a blank cheque.

The President of the Third Republic, Raymond Poincaré, and the Prime Minister, René Viviani, were in St Petersburg from 20 to 23 July. Sarajevo was discussed and a warning to Austria–Hungary considered, but the ultimatum was deliberately delivered after their departure and the Germans tried to jam radio communications with the presidential vessel. Between the 23rd and Poincaré's and Viviani's return to Paris on the 29th, contact with them was poor and unreliable. However, far from inhibiting a forceful Franco-Russian response to Austria–Hungary it instead facilitated one, by allowing greater leeway to more subordinate figures. During Poincaré's and Viviani's absence from Paris the

French War Minister and the CGS told the Russian military attaché of their optimism about the prospects in a conflict and reminded Russia of its pledges to attack Germany at once if war erupted – which would rule out a partial mobilisation against the Dual Monarchy. The Ambassador in St Petersburg, Maurice Paléologue, told Sazonov before the 24 July Council of Ministers that 'France would not only give Russia strong diplomatic support but would, if necessary, fulfil all the obligations imposed on her by the alliance' [3: no. 68].

If war was coming, Paléologue, like the French military, was determined that Russia should attack as early as possible, and he probably gave more unequivocal assurances than Poincaré and Viviani would have done, as well as being slow to tell Paris about what Russia was up to. After Poincaré and Viviani returned they telegraphed on 30 July urging Russia to do nothing that might make Germany mobilise, but the message arrived too late to halt the general mobilisation decree. Strictly speaking, by not properly consulting their partners the Russians could be said to have contravened the alliance, and the French could have used this pretext to abandon them. Poincaré and Viviani were clear, however, that rather than do so they would face war, and when Germany required them to pledge neutrality they refused [99; 100; 102; 104].

If this seems paradoxical, it should be remembered why the alliance was concluded in the first place: if Russia were beaten, France alone would be hard pressed to defy German threats or to repel a German invasion. In many ways Paléologue and the military were simply following the trend of French policy since Agadir, a leading theme of which was the 'national reawakening' or *réveil national*. Jean-Jacques Becker has underscored the limits to the nationalist revival, which was most intense among the Paris intellectual and political elite. Parliamentary elections in May–June 1914 showed a swing to the Left. All the same, commentators at the time believed that the *réveil* was real, and that government policy reflected it [97].

One indication came in strategic planning, with the adoption under the new CGS, General Joseph Joffre, of Plan XVII, under which the French army would open a war by immediately invading German territory [51; 55]. Poincaré, who became Premier and Foreign Minister in 1912, sought to rally national confidence and heighten military and diplomatic preparedness. Elected President in the following year, he retained a guiding influence on external policy. It is not true that he wished to start a war in order to recover Alsace-Lorraine, lost to Germany in 1871. None the less, he did want to make the Triple Entente strong enough to deter an attack, and to defeat one if deterrence failed. Arms were sold and loans extended in the Balkans. Military contacts with St Petersburg were stepped up, Russia having promised in 1911 to attack Germany on Day 15 of mobilisation. The Three-Year Law was not only an answer to Germany's bill but was also needed to complement Plan XVII and reassure Nicholas II. Although the Franco-Russian Alliance, like the Austro-German one, was defensive, in 1912 Poincaré apparently promised assistance to the Russians if they were attacked by Germany because of involvement in an Austro-Serb conflict. This undertaking paralleled Germany's reinterpretation in 1909 of its commitment to Vienna, and set a further precedent for 1914 [100–3].

French activism before Sarajevo helps explain why the Central Powers felt so pressured. With the crucial exception of policy toward Russia, however, the French were studiedly cautious during the July Crisis. Joffre did not push for war, but he feared being caught unprepared, and yet ministers resisted his pleas for more precautions. Poincaré may have feared that the Three-Year Law would soon be watered down because of the Left's election successes [101], but in general France like Russia had an interest in postponing a showdown. There was therefore a fear of provoking one unnecessarily, and there were two special reasons for restraint. The first was public opinion, the new nationalism being offset by the growth of the socialist vote, while the main trade-union federation, the CGT, was committed to a general strike against war. The government persuaded the socialists that France was the victim of unprovoked aggression, and successfully gambled that it need not arrest the left-wingers who were listed as potential saboteurs in the so-called 'B note' (*Carnet B*). The assassination of the socialist leader Jean Jaurès by a royalist fanatic on 31 July helped rally the CGT to the war effort [97].

The second reason for restraint was Britain. The French were uncertain where it stood until the final stages, and to win Britain over it was vital to appear the innocent party. For this reason Plan XVII, unlike the Schlieffen–Moltke Plan, excluded an immediate invasion of Belgium. The French delayed reinforcing their frontier, and on 30 July ordered their troops to stay ten kilometres behind it, again with London in mind. Although they could not force Britain to help them, they so managed the crisis as to raise no obstacles to its doing so [55].

4   Towards World War

We now come to Germany's decision to start a European war. It came on 31 July, with the ultimata to St Petersburg and Paris and the proclamation of the *Kriegsgefahrzustand*, or 'Condition of Danger of War', a state of alert and preparation similar to Russia's pre-mobilisation measures, which was followed by general mobilisation on 1 August. In contrast to the blank cheque, this decision followed three days of hesitation and debate, not least because it was understood to mean hostilities not just against Russia and France but almost certainly against Britain.

Events between 28 and 30 July exposed the superficiality of the consensus among the German leaders established at the start of the crisis. When Wilhelm returned from his cruise he tried to back off. Early on the 28th he wrote to Bethmann that Serbia's reply removed all need for war, and suggested that the Austrians should halt in Belgrade, just across the border, holding the city as a guarantee that Serbia would honour its pledges. But Bethmann had no intention of being so deflected, and in communicating Wilhelm's message he stripped it of much of its force, saying that he did not wish to hold Vienna back so much as to avoid a world war, and if one came anyway to make Russia seem to blame. On the 29th, however, he too changed tack, urging Austria-Hungary to accept the 'Halt in Belgrade' arrangement, which was now also being proposed by Britain. Although Fischer has questioned his sincerity there seems no reason to doubt it, and there are persuasive explanations of his behaviour [3: nos 112, 115, 130, 133].

The first was German public opinion. The authorities were in contact with the SPD leaders, who were willing to accept mobilisation if the government did not repress them and St Petersburg was clearly the aggressor [123]. Second, Marc Trachtenberg has suggested that impending Russian partial mobilisation made

Bethmann hesitate, but according to Jack Levy the principal influence (and certainly the one the Chancellor cited to the Austrians) was a belated warning from Sir Edward Grey on 29 July that Britain would quickly intervene in a Franco-German conflict. If Levy is right, it would support Fischer's insistence that the Germans gave the blank cheque in a mistaken expectation of British neutrality. This implies that an earlier British warning might have led them to restrain Vienna while Russian preparations were less advanced and there was less pressure of time [48; 53].

Anglo-German relations have remained among the most disputed aspects of the crisis, and Luigi Albertini, among others, condemned Grey for not acting sooner [9]. The evidence is contradictory. Britain had supported France in both Moroccan Crises, in the second via a public declaration in the July 1911 Mansion House Speech by the Chancellor of the Exchequer, David Lloyd George. The 'War Council' had followed another warning that Britain would assist France in a struggle with Germany. But since 1912 Anglo-German relations had improved, and the Germans may have believed that the entente ties were weakening. By the spring of 1914, Tirpitz, Jagow and the Foreign Ministry's chief British expert, Wilhelm von Stumm, were optimistic that London might stay neutral. On the other hand, Fischer's critics have emphasised the depression caused in Berlin by the Anglo-Russian naval discussions, which suggested that encirclement was tightening its grip. A possible reconciliation between these viewpoints may be that after moving away from its partners Britain seemed about to move closer again, which strengthened the case for resolving matters now. Furthermore, Grey's initial caution in the crisis probably encouraged German illusions. He implied to the German Ambassador, Prince Lichnowsky, that Britain would stay out of a war involving 'four' Continental Powers, and on 23 July Bethmann advised Wilhelm that 'it is improbable that England will immediately come into the fray' [127: p. 63]. By the 29th the Chancellor was confident enough to make a crass neutrality bid, offering not to annex Belgian territory (which was practically admitting that Germany meant to invade) or French territory in Europe (though not overseas) if Britain kept out. The bid crossed with Lichnowsky's telegram reporting Grey's warning, on receiving which the

29

Chancellor belatedly tried to put his diplomatic machine into reverse gear [96; 142].

Like Poincaré's and Viviani's appeal to Russia on 30 July, Bethman's appeal to Austria–Hungary came very late in the day. Turner and Trachtenberg have questioned the idea that it failed because it was undermined by Moltke [53–4]. It is true that on the 30th Moltke telegraphed to Conrad, urging him to mobilise against Russia and saying Germany would do likewise. As Joffre feared a Russian concentration against Austria–Hungary, Moltke feared an Austrian one against Serbia, which indeed was what Conrad had already begun. Moltke's action exceeded his authority (though he may have had Wilhelm's approval for it), and made it easier for Berchtold to reject Bethmann's pleas. But before Berchtold's reply arrived Bethmann had already decided during the night of 30/31 July to call off his initiative, the chief reason being the overwhelming evidence now arriving of French and Belgian as well as Russian military measures, in the light of which Moltke joined the War Minister, Erich von Falkenhayn, in pressing for the *Kriegsgefahrzustand*. The Chancellor conceded that there must be a decision in any event by midday on the 31st, but confirmation arrived that morning of Russia's general mobilisation, giving him the pretext that he needed to blame St Petersburg and to carry the SPD [136; 141].

The preparations made by Belgium and the Entente Powers, especially Russia, were the immediate reason for Germany's actions. This does not, however, vindicate Bethmann's apologias that Russian mobilisation had destroyed his peace initiative, that the crisis had got out of control, and that no government had wanted war. If Germany had stood by while its enemies got ready, the Schlieffen–Moltke Plan would have become inoperable and it would have had to choose between military suicide and diplomatic humiliation. But this was a dilemma that Berlin itself had Pargely created. Although there were two days of conflict on 29–30 July while Bethmann requested delay until he could put Russia in the wrong, there was much common ground between civilians and military. Bethmann and Jagow were ignorant of the details of the Schlieffen–Moltke Plan (including the seizure of Liège), but they understood it in outline, and the pressure that Germany would face once the Triple Entente started preparing. War against Russia and France was a contingency they had reckoned with from the start. No German leader, on the other hand, wanted war with Britain, although Moltke seems to have been indifferent about whether London came in. As late as 1 August, the Chancellor and Wilhelm jumped at a report that Grey was willing to stay aloof, and for a few hours they suspended the march to the west, overriding the CGS's protests. When the news proved misleading, they let operations go ahead. This incident – the so-called 'misunderstanding' – demonstrates that the Emperor and the civilians rather than the military were in charge; but its outcome underlines that they too would accept the likelihood of war with Britain in preference to doing nothing while France and Russia armed [53; 91; 96].

If it is not true that the German authorities 'lost control' or were dictated to by Moltke, they certainly displayed outstanding incompetence. Having misjudged Russia's commitment to Serbia and Britain's to France, they went to war with little idea of how to defeat either Power. Even against France, it now seems that although the General Staff expected early successes they were unsure about whether a decisive victory was possible [121]. Nor did the Germans think much about their war aims and about exactly how using force would solve their difficulties. It is true that Bethmann's neutrality bid betrayed his interest in French colonies, and on 31 July Wilhelm said that Russia must lose Poland. African expansion and a Central European customs union had been under consideration in the Chancellery since at least 1912, although in January 1914 the government had agreed that Germany's existing customs tariffs were satisfactory [16, 1st edn: chs 3, 5]. These straws in the wind, as well as the speed, once hostilities broke out, with which work began on war aims, suggest that Fischer is right to suppose that the government had some idea of what it wanted, and the July Crisis was not simply a preventive manoeuvre against encirclement. But this does not mean that Germany went to war in a premeditated bid for World-Power status. The decision-making in July was incremental and reactive: first a decision to use the Sarajevo pretext to start a local war and risk a Continental one; then a further decision to open hostilities with Russia and France; and from this latter decision the ultimatum to Brussels and the breach with London followed. The German leaders felt that they were acting defensively against encirclement and a deteriorating military balance, as well as propping up their ally. But their means of self-defence was attack, and their solution to their problems, though still waiting to be worked out, was Continental and global expansion.

Germany's decisions meant there would be war between the Austro-German and Franco-Russian blocs. Of the two semi-detached Powers Italy opted provisionally for neutrality, although Austro-Hungary's and Germany's brinkmanship had been encouraged by their expectation that Italy might assist them [70: ch. 2; 148]. The Italian military and naval chiefs had recently made contingency plans with their partners, but the Foreign Minister and Premier, the Marquis di San Giuliano and Antonio Salandra, preferred, with the support of King Victor Emmanuel III, not to implement them. Italy's defensive obligations under the Triple Alliance did not apply if Austria–Hungary attacked Serbia, especially as Vienna had ignored its obligation under Article VII of the treaty to agree with Italy on compensation before embarking on Balkan operations. San Giuliano still offered to help in return for Italian-speaking territory in the Trentino, but Vienna refused to make promises. In any case, the Italians (who had ambitions of their own in Albania), had no interest in seeing Habsburg power grow, and they feared becoming a satellite of a victorious Germany. They dreaded a war against the British fleet, which could cut off their imports, take their colonies, and bombard their cities. The Libyan war had stretched government finances and halted rearmament, and there was severe social unrest. Given all these reasons, it seemed wise for Italy to stay out of the conflict, at least until it was clearer which side would win. In May 1915, lured by offers of Austrian territory and expecting an early victory, Rome finally declared war on Vienna, only to find that it had signed up for three years of attrition [145–7].

Like the Italian Government, the British one did not feel bound to intervene. Although Britain had signed the Treaty of London of 1839, guaranteeing Belgium's independence, it was disputed whether the United Kingdom was obliged to assist by force of arms if another signatory violated the guarantee, and on 29 July the Cabinet agreed that any decision to help Belgium would be 'rather one of policy than legal obligation' [24: p. 36]. As for Britain's relationships with France and Russia, the 1904 and 1907 ententes had concerned extra-European disputes, although with France Britain had also concluded a military cooperation agreement in 1911 and a naval one in 1913. The former provided for up to six divisions of the British Expeditionary Force (BEF) to be shipped across the Channel to fight alongside the French army. The second provided that in wartime the French fleet would look after the western Mediterranean and the British the eastern Mediterranean and the English Channel east of the Isle of Wight, including the northern French coast. But a secret exchange of letters between Grey and the French Ambassador, Paul Cambon, in November 1912, specified that these were purely contingency agreements. If peace were threatened the two Powers would consult, and if they decided on joint military action they could take the plans into account. In practice, they were likely to use them rather than to improvise, but there was no undertaking to do so. The French army draw up Plan XVII without assuming British help; the navy redeployed towards the Mediterranean in 1912, leaving the Channel potentially exposed, but it had fallback plans for fighting alone. In 1914 Britain was committed to consultation but to no more [55; 95].

None the less, on Sunday 2 August the British Cabinet resolved to protect the French coast and fleet, and the German navy was warned to keep out of the Channel. In fact it was willing to stay out anyway. But the Cabinet also resolved to protect Belgium against a 'substantial' violation of its neutrality. This resolution was followed by the ultimatum to Germany and by Britain's declaration of war.

In the first phase of the crisis the Liberal Government was still preoccupied with the storm aroused by its Irish Home Rule Bill, which threatened to cause civil war between nationalists in Dublin and loyalists in Belfast. European diplomacy was left to the Foreign Office. After 27 July, however, the Cabinet was in near continuous discussion of Continental developments, and until close to the end the majority opposed intervention. As late as 1 August it was decided in no circumstances to send the BEF, and Grey told Cambon that France must make its own decision on whether or not to help Russia, with no assurance of British support. What tipped the balance on the 2nd was, on one level, party political dynamics. Grey warned that if no promises were made to France and Belgium he would resign; and the Prime Minister, Herbert Asquith, said he would go with him. The leaders of the Unionist (i.e. Conservative) opposition urged support for France and Russia. If the neutralists persisted, the government seemed likely to break up and a coalition of Unionists and interventionist Liberals was likely to take Britain in anyway. It was preferable to keep the Cabinet united and in office, so that liberal principles could be safeguarded against patriotic excesses, and ministers protect their careers. The most plausible leader of a non-interventionist revolt, Lloyd George, supported Asquith, and only two Cabinet members resigned [80; 90; 92].

Party politics, however, can give only an incomplete explanation without reference to the underlying issues. Even without a treaty obligation, Belgium mattered. For centuries English policy had striven to keep the Low Countries, opposite London and the Thames estuary, outside the control of a hostile Power, and it was for this reason that the 1839 treaty had been signed in the first place. If this national security consideration influenced the Right, for the Left there were moral issues of upholding small nations and the rule of law, and showing that aggression did not pay. It was uncertain whether Belgium would resist invasion, especially a passage merely through the south-eastern tip of the country, the Ardennes. But Germany's brutal ultimatum, the Brussels Government's courageous rejection of it, and King Albert's appeal for assistance, removed all ambiguity [12: ch. 7].

Without the invasion Britain's entry would certainly have been less prompt and more contested, and might not have happened at all. In contrast to the Franco-Prussian War of 1870–1, however, the British would not have been content simply to let the two sides slug it out, so long as Belgium was respected. The commitment to Brussels was not an even-handed one against all comers, and had the French broken the treaty it is inconceivable that Britain would have fought them. The invasion mattered because Germany was the invader, and most of the British political elite had decided that Germany should not be allowed to defeat the French. This applied not only to the Unionists and to Asquith, Grey, and Winston Churchill, the leading Cabinet interventionists, but also to Lloyd George [77]. 'It is against British interests', wrote Asquith on 24 July, 'that France should be wiped out as a Great Power' [12: p. 145].

No such vital interest was recognised in Eastern Europe, and as late as 1 August Grey was attracted by the option of neutrality if

France and Germany stayed at peace, leaving Russia to face the Central Powers alone [91]. He hesitated to commit himself, as Sazonov wanted, to a joint declaration in support of Serbia. Yet, as Keith Wilson has demonstrated, the implications for a neutral Britain if France and Russia won might be little better than if Germany did. It had concluded the ententes because it lacked the strength to defend its worldwide interests against multiple dangers, and not initially to contain Berlin (with whom, in 1898–1901, it had tried unsuccessfully to negotiate an alliance), although containing Germany later became a supplementary objective. The Russian entente was an alternative to a ruinously expensive fortification programme on the north-west Indian frontier that would have cut into social reform and battleship building while probably still leaving India vulnerable to invasion. But friction with St Petersburg persisted, and in Persia by 1914 it was reaching dangerous levels, Grey commenting in June that Anglo-Russian relations were in 'crisis'. On 25 July Sazonov warned that if Britain remained uncommitted it would jeopardise the Russian friendship that it needed in Asia, and this may have caused Grey to side more definitely with his partners. Similarly, Paul Cambon warned that Anglo-French hostility might also revive [28: ch. 7; 93; 94].

All the same, Anglo-German antagonism was real enough, quite apart from Britain's need to get along with France and Russia, and it was the German danger that weighed most with the Cabinet. According to Paul Kennedy and Zara Steiner, the antagonism had five elements [82; 90]. The first was ideological, Britain in most ways having more liberal institutions, but it is doubtful whether this contributed much, and the second – commercial rivalry – was more acute at the turn of the century than during the subsequent trade boom. German exports of steel, chemicals, and machinery were generally more competitive than British ones, and made inroads into the British home market. German tariff increases, in 1879 and 1902, had been condemned as discriminatory. None the less, in the 1906 general election the Liberals achieved a landslide victory on a platform of maintaining free trade. The two countries remained among each other's best customers, and although Britain ran a trade deficit with Germany the empire as a whole had a balance of payments surplus. Tariff protectionism helped push the Unionists in an anti-German direction, but on the whole commercial rivalry was not a major issue on the eve of war.

Rivalry outside Europe, the third source of friction, was also greater at the turn of the century than during the pre-1914 détente. German *Weltpolitik* (for example, Wilhelm's support for the Boers in South Africa) had provoked the British at a sensitive moment when they felt over-extended and their nineteenth-century pre-eminence was fading [76]. However, Bethmann was willing to pursue his African objectives through negotiation, and Grey saw this as an area where he could appease his Radical critics and reduce tension. An agreement reached in 1914 demarcated zones of railway building in the Ottoman Empire, protecting Britain's special position in the Persian Gulf. A 1913 understanding revised one of 1898 that defined the share-out of the spoils if Portugal's African empire broke up: but it was never confirmed, as the Germans objected to Britain's wish to publish it simultaneously with an 1899 treaty guaranteeing the Portuguese empire's integrity [84]. This cynical episode underlined the limits to Britain's willingness to be accommodating: but at least colonial issues were open to discussion.

The same was not true of the fourth and fifth issues: naval rivalry and the European balance of power. Bethmann had earlier tried to link these issues, but the two sides got down to discussing detail only during the Haldane Mission in February 1912, when the Secretary of State for War travelled to Berlin. During Haldane's visit Germany announced another navy bill, increasing the proportion of its fleet kept at readiness. Britain offered a promise of non-aggression – that neither side would attack the other – but refused to pledge neutrality in a Continental conflict. After the failure of the Mission, the main initiative in 1912–13 was the proposal by Winston Churchill (the First Lord of the Admiralty) for a one-year 'naval holiday' or freeze on new building. This would benefit Britain, whose shipyards could easily find alternative orders, more than Germany, and it led nowhere. Yet despite the stalemate, the naval race was losing impetus as the Germans concentrated on their army, and the ratio between the fleets was approximating to one that both sides could live with. The British were pushed hard, but kept the advantage; Tirpitz's new dreadnoughts made him feel less vulnerable to a preventive strike. Although the naval race did more than anything else to form British perceptions of Germany as an enemy, the fact that negotiations stalled may actually have eased tension by sidelining the most emotive issue [83; 86].

This underlines, however, the limitations of the Anglo-German détente, which represented only a superficial improvement in the relationship. Paul Kennedy has contended that the most serious source of antagonism was economic, not because of competition for trade, but because Germany's wealth and population might enable it – as had no Power since Napoleon – to dominate the Continent [82: pp. 464–5]. This is true with the proviso (as Kennedy acknowledges) that American growth was even more dramatic, yet perceived in Britain to be less threatening. Germany combined expanding resources with geographical proximity and, under Wilhelm II, with disturbing and unpredictable behaviour. British statesmen were determined, while using the détente to keep friction below danger point, to deny Berlin a free hand against France and Russia and to preserve a balance of power. Each side, in fact, entered the July Crisis under misapprehensions about the other's allegiances. The Germans underestimated Britain's commitment to French independence. But Grey thought he could co-operate with Bethmann as in 1912 to rein in Austria–Hungary, and the Germans may have played on this by encouraging him to suppose that a struggle between hawks and doves was in progress, in which he needed to help the latter [74]. This, rather than his difficulties in Cabinet, may explain Grey's delay in warning Berlin, and his later anger against Germany arose partly from a sense of having been deceived.

So far the emphasis has been on the political elite. George V lacked the influence of his Continental counterparts, as did the military and naval chiefs. The army's Director of Military Operations, Sir Henry Wilson, failed to commit the government to mobilising the BEF. Although the Royal Navy was kept at heightened readiness and sent to battle stations in Scapa Flow, this was undertaken by Churchill, in liaison with Grey and Asquith, rather than at the behest of the admirals. On the other hand, Parliament's approval for war was essential, but once the Unionists had shown their colours and Radical opposition had evaporated, it was not difficult to obtain. The evidence of patriotic feeling on the streets of London and in the press helped the politicians to close ranks, but there is little more evidence than in

Germany that the authorities went to war in order to consolidate the existing order at home. With regard to the situation in Ireland, Asquith felt that the European crisis might distract attention from Home Rule and extract him from a virtually insoluble dilemma. However, although this served as a compensation it can hardly be seen as a motive for intervention. Moreover, Britain had just undergone an unprecedented strike wave, and the recent formation of a 'triple alliance' of miners, dockers, and railwaymen promised worse. The expectation was that war, so far from stabilising society, would bring food shortages and would intensify working-class unrest. Two divisions of the Expeditionary Force were initially kept at home as a precaution [75; 90].

The Cabinet's decision-making rested on certain assumptions about the kind of war it would fight, even if these were not examined very rigorously. Wilson had advised that the two sides were evenly matched, so that quick intervention might tilt the scales in the West and sustain French morale. None the less, ministers made up their minds on 2 August having resolved on the previous day that the BEF would not be sent at all, a sub-committee dominated by interventionists reversing this decision only after hostilities were declared. At all events, the military operations were expected to be brief, and France and Russia to take most of the casualties, perhaps weakening them to Britain's advantage while German trade and colonies were mopped up. Churchill was confident of the navy's superiority, and if the struggle lasted longer he and Grey knew of the Admiralty's estimate that, whatever the short-term disruption to British shipping, Germany was much more vulnerable to blockade. Like the other Powers, the British committed themselves with little inkling of what lay in store for them [39; 78; 80].

5 The Search for Understanding

So far this study has surveyed the state of historical understanding of the decisions taken in each capital in 1914. From here on, it will turn to the problem of generalisation. It is time to stand back from the march of events and to isolate the characteristics of pre-war Europe as a whole that led it over the brink. As a preliminary, we need to clarify how our present understanding was obtained, considering both the evidence available and the concerns with which historians have interpreted it.

Given the catastrophic consequences of the July Crisis, it is not surprising that it has attracted an immense body of literature. Moreover, exceptional quantities of information about the crisis became available unprecedently soon after the event. Within weeks of the outbreak of war the belligerents published selections from their archives in the so-called 'coloured books'. The deluge of statemen's memoirs that followed the conflict included some, such as those of Churchill, Grey, Poincaré, and Conrad [63; 72; 79; 102], that were highly revealing. But above all, what made the topic an exceptional field for investigation were the multi-volume collections of Foreign Ministry documents that began appearing in the 1920s. The Bolsheviks began the process after seizing power in 1917, with revelations from the tsarist files. More material appeared in the journal *Red Archive* and the massive *International Relations in the Era of Imperialism* [5]. The interim government set up in Berlin after Wilhelm II abdicated in November 1918 commissioned the veteran socialist Karl Kautsky to edit what became four volumes on the July Crisis, translated as *Outbreak of the World War* [8]. They were followed by 40 volumes on the pre-war period, *Die Grosse Politik der europäischen Kabinette* [7], which prompted the Austrians and Germany's former enemies to follow suit, if only to show that they had nothing to hide [1; 2; 4; 6]. The *Grosse Politik*, especially, had a polemical purpose, and has to be used cautiously. All the collections are more informative on diplomacy than on the economic, ideological, or strategic aspects of Great-Power relations, and they help to explain why writing on war origins focused for so long on topics such as alliances and crises. None the less, they allowed historians to retrace events almost from hour to hour, and their appearance marked the first of two revolutions in the accessibility of evidence.

The second revolution was the opening of the European archives. The German ones were the earliest to enter the public domain, through being captured by the 1945 victors, although most of the military records had been bombed. The British and Austrian papers were released in the 1960s, and the French and Italian ones soon afterwards. Soviet archives were opened selectively to Western scholars during the 1970s détente: the collapse of Communism may lead to important new discoveries in Moscow, not to mention Belgrade. Historians can now compare the selections published between the wars with the original files, and broaden their enquiry from Foreign Ministry material to army, navy, and financial papers or to the minutes of co-ordinating bodies such as the Austro-Hungarian Joint Council of Ministers and the British Committee of Imperial Defence. They can turn to private letters and diaries and to the documents left by non-governmental agencies such as political parties, business associations, and pressure groups. These developments have made it possible to reorientate the study of foreign policy, and to relocate it in the context of the societies from which the policy emanated.

The study of war origins has been shaped not only by the source material but also by the preoccupations of the writers who have used it. Between the wars the most important work was conducted in the shadow of Article 231. Reparations dominated politics not only in Germany but also in France, where Poincaré ordered troops into the Ruhr in 1923, and his critics tried to brand him as a warmonger. In the United States the resurgence of isolationism was linked with efforts to prove that both sides in the war had been as bad as each other and that capitalist machinations had drawn America into a senseless slaughter [17]. All of this prepared the ground for the revisionists, of whom the most

40

influential were probably Harry Barnes and Sidney Fay [10; 13]. As against them, Pierre Renouvin and Bernadotte Schmitt, while not going as far as the Versailles Treaty, reaffirmed the Central Powers' primary share of the blame [21; 22].

These accounts relied heavily on the published documents, and to begin with mainly on the *Grosse Politik*, as the Allied editions were slower to appear. They were superseded by Luigi Albertini's enormous three-volume study of *The Origins of the War of 1914* [9], which originally appeared in Italy during the Second World War, but had its biggest influence only after being translated. Based on extraordinarily intensive study of all the documentary collections, as well as on memoirs and interviews, it reconstructed the July Crisis with a thoroughness that is unlikely to be surpassed. Though criticising all the Powers, and stressing the roles of mis-understanding and of civilian unfamiliarity with military consider-ations, it attributed special responsibility to Germany and to the Schlieffen–Moltke Plan. With this exception, however, the 1950s marked a pause, and it was Fritz Fischer's first volume in 1961 that started the next phase. Apart from reopening the debate on German responsibility, Fischer and his disciples rode the crest of the wave of the second evidence revolution (the September Programme, for example, emerging from the East German archives). Whereas earlier writers up to Albertini had tended to study the international system as a whole, the new emphasis was on the national unit and the domestic roots of foreign policy. During the 1970s and 1980s the approach was imitated elsewhere, and similar, if less vociferous, debates emerged about domestic factors in the other Powers, though few writers emphasised them as much as did Fischer. On the other hand, during the resur-gence of superpower tension under Presidents Carter and Reagan, American political scientists and historians showed revived interest in the pre-1914 international system, reacting against Fischer's domestic focus in favour of comparative and the-matic studies of war plans, intelligence, and armaments [27; 47–53]. The underlying issue in this literature was that of how far war was inadvertent, or generated by the system, and how far gov-ernments willed it. Finally, against the uncertain backdrop of the 1990s, attention seems to be shifting again, to topics such as nationalism, economic integration, and cultural determinants of power politics [39; 44; 57; 58; 60].

The Fischer controversy and the second evidence revolution have so widened the research agenda and swelled the flow of publications that it is ever harder to attempt a synthesis. James Joll's is the best available, and John Langdon's survey of the historiography is an invaluable complement [15; 17]. Given the vast extension of our knowledge of the problem, and the new theoretical formulations of it, what conclusions may be drawn about the reasons for the war?

Recent trends in the debate have clarified the question of whether or not 1914 was a war by accident, and the related problem of responsibility [50: ch. 8; 53]. To say, with the French and German historians in 1951, that no government or people had a premeditated desire for war, blurs the issues. It is more accurate to see statesmen entering the crisis with alternative scenarios and hierarchies of preference, among which various kinds of war were certainly included, if not necessarily those most strongly favoured. Policies were compromises between diverging views, and we must differentiate from country to country. For France and Britain, making up their minds late in the crisis, the choice was whether to leave their partners to be beaten, and whether they could live with a victorious Germany. Both answered no, and in this sense it is true that they opted for war. But they would have preferred not to have faced the dilemma, which was forced on them by Austria–Hungary and Germany and to an extent by Russia, who took the essential decisions while there still remained some room for manoeuvre.

New research has confirmed the Austrians' determination to use force against Serbia and that they saw little chance of avoiding war with St Petersburg [65; 70–1]. Sazonov and Nicholas II, on the other hand, in resolving to stand by Belgrade, hoped to avoid a conflict with the Central Powers but were willing to fight rather than give way. They eventually ordered general mobilisation in the conviction that their opponents' refusal to yield made bloodshed inevitable. Germany remains the most difficult case, partly because of the lack of policy co-ordination. Moltke wanted a Continental war, and expected, if Britain came in, to see off the BEF without difficulty. Wilhelm wanted and predicted a localised Austro-Serb struggle, and tried half-heartedly to stop it escalating, though he accepted that if Russia mobilised he would have to retaliate. The most plausible interpretation of Bethmann

Hollweg's conduct, despite the lack of corroborating evidence, remains that he was taking a 'calculated risk' or placing a two-way bet. He left it to St Petersburg to decide whether the fighting would remain localised or would spread, even if he worked for and preferred the former outcome. While he was correct in saying that the Chancellor did not want or foresee immediate British entry, Fischer went too far in arguing that Sarajevo was simply a pretext for a war against France and Russia that had already been decided on. It remains true that in German military circles there was enthusiasm for a major conflict now, and that Vienna and Berlin took the initiative in forcing peace/war decisions on the Triple Entente. Primary responsibility should rightly be attributed to the Central Powers, and although the Austrians had justified grounds for thinking that their Serbian and Russian enemies wished to destroy them, this does not seem true of Entente object-ives against Germany, however, threatening they may have seemed to Berlin at the time.

None the less, inadvertence and miscalculation played a part in the crisis. The Russians underestimated the impact of their pre-mobilisation measures; Bethmann misjudged Britain. The crisis might have ended peacefully if Grey had warned Germany earlier and Germany had held back Austria–Hungary, especially if there had been parallel French restraint of Russia. But somebody – or everybody – would have had to give ground, although the stakes were much higher than in previous confrontations and both sides were courting the danger of war. Even if powers miscalculated, what was significant was their readiness to gamble with lives. Attempts to probe the roots of this new bellicosity have been of two main kinds: those emphasising internal factors, and those emphasising international ones. In truth, the two approaches are interconnected and there is no need to rely exclusively on one or the other, although for the sake of clarity each will be examined in turn.

Decisions for war were facilitated by the lack of domestic resist-ance. German, French, and British leaders wanted public approval, even a military man such as Moltke acknowledging the value of a rallying cry and of national consensus. Contrary to expectation, opposition collapsed with barely a struggle, partly because most of the leaders of the Left were not uncompromising anti-militarists. In Britain, Churchill and Lloyd George had

43

opposed higher dreadnought spending in 1909, but agreed after the Agadir Crisis that France could not be allowed to go under. The Radicals lost influence after the Liberal majority dwindled in the 1910 elections, and even an increasingly assertive trade-union movement was unwilling to embrace strike action against hostilities. All of these considerations assisted Asquith and Grey [77; 87; 90].

But it was on the Continent where the anti-war movement appeared strongest. The Second International, emerging in 1889 from an initiative by German, French, and British representatives to co-ordinate the policies and actions of the world socialist movement, seemed the wave of the future. Membership of its affiliated organisations rose from 2.4 to 4.1 million between 1900 and 1914. Germany and France had the largest socialist parties, the SPD and the SFIO, both of which campaigned for peace during the First Balkan War and opposed the 1913 army bills, despite the SPD's support for the capital levy used to finance the German measure. Socialist representatives met in periodic congresses (most recently at Basle in 1912), and the International's secretariat could convene the party leaders to meet as the International Socialist Bureau (ISB), which they did in Brussels on 28–9 July 1914. None the less, peace demonstrations in Europe's cities ended in late July, to be superseded by cheering patriotic crowds [97; 143]. Political truces were formed in every belligerent (except Russia and Serbia), socialists voted war credits, and sometimes entered cabinets. Strikes on the railways and in the arms plants might have obstructed mobilisation, and there could have been appeals to ignore the call-up, yet in the event resistance was negligible [30; 32].

The International was a valuable co-ordinating device if the member parties wished to use it, but it had no powers of direction or discipline. And if there was agreement on the diagnosis of the problem there was little on an effective remedy. The official position of the organisation, set out in the Stuttgart resolution of 1907, was that war was the product of capitalism and only by abolishing capitalism could it be ended. If hostilities threatened before then, however, each party was left to decide what to do, the Germans opposing a prior commitment to strike action. Although the German trade-union movement was one of the strongest in Europe, this, paradoxically, became part of the problem, for if a strike were called Germany's war effort would suffer more than elsewhere. Conversely, with the decision left to each country the more militant French trade unions were the most likely to act, in which case France would be disproportionately disadvantaged.

These considerations might not matter if the workers really had no fatherland, but in practice they behaved as if they did. The doctrine inherited from Marx and Engels was not pacifist but judged wars according to whether they were historically progressive. From the SPD's standpoint, a Russian victory would benefit reaction; from the SFIO's, a German one would do likewise. Both the SPD and the SFIO were ready to accept a war in the name of self-defence, and to both parties this was what 1914 seemed to be. The CGT recognised no such distinction – all wars slaughtered the workers — but they felt little in common with their German counterparts. Finally, the socialist leaders seem to have been lulled into a false sense of security by the peaceful resolution of so many crises in 1911–13. The ISB meeting on 28–9 July put off reaching any decisions until an emergency congress, scheduled for 12 August in Vienna. The French trade unionists sounded out the Germans and found them unwilling to move. The Vienna Congress never assembled, and by 12 August socialist solidarity had evaporated [30; 31; 32].

To say that European governments were able to marginalise the Left is not to argue that they went to war to buttress the status quo [29; 33]. The requirements of domestic stabilisation did influence foreign policy, but more subtly. German *Weltpolitik* and naval construction were intended to win approbation for the Hohenzollern dynasty [105]. Britain, it has been argued, needed the ententes in part to release resources at home [94]. But these were background considerations, which may have helped to set Berlin and London on a collision course but did not predetermine war. In 1914 the Power that best fitted the counter-revolutionary model may have been Russia, where Sazonov urged firmness on Nicholas in order to head off insurrection, but by insurrection he meant not Bolshevism but a Pan-Slav reaction against a Balkan humiliation. The Tsar disregarded the memorandum submitted to him in February by the former Interior Minister, Peter Durnovo, who predicted that war would lead to anarchy [155: pp. 77–83]. The Austro-Hungarian leaders certainly feared that nationalism (rather than socialism) would break up their empire, but they expected the precipitant to be invasion rather than internal revolt. In France, despite the tradition of rebellion, there is no evidence that the fear of it influenced the government in the July Crisis. On the contrary, it was confident enough to set aside *Carnet B*. In Britain, Asquith hoped to avert civil strife across the Irish Sea, but war entry was not expected to defuse working-class unrest: rather the opposite. In Germany, too, though some called for war as a means of domestic consolidation, Bethmann feared that it would subvert the monarchy, and the advocates of a *Flucht nach Vorn* interpretation have not proved their case (cf. p. 12 above).

An alternative interpretation of the interconnection between foreign and domestic policy was given by Lenin. In his *Imperialism, the Highest Stage of Capitalism*, written in 1916, he argued that since 1900 capitalism had entered a new and more aggressive phase, in which ownership was concentrated and banks held a controlling position. Markets for goods mattered less than did outlets for investment, and 'uneven development', or unequal growth rates, undermined international equilibrium. The world war was a struggle to redistribute spheres of influence, and the prizes included not only underdeveloped areas but Europe itself [38].

Lenin's account of the roots of imperialism is the shakiest part of his analysis. It is true that industry in some countries was becoming more oligopolistic, and that there already existed a 'military–industrial complex', in President Eisenhower's later phrase, of armaments firms dependent on exports and on government contracts. It is much harder to demonstrate that business interests determined foreign policies, especially as businessmen were divided among themselves. The arms firms were not strong enough on their own to start the land arms race, and it was not necessarily in their interest to do so. Krupp of Essen, the biggest weapons manufacturer in Europe, had invested heavily in capacity for producing warship guns and armour, and when German priorities shifted to the army the firm's profitability suffered. As for financial interests, the spectre of war caused panic on the Berlin Bourse in 1911 and the London Stock Exchange in 1914, while the Director of the Creditanstalt bank in Vienna, which controlled much of the Habsburg defence industry, urged in vain after Sarajevo that Austria–Hungary should settle with Serbia peacefully [52]. Fischer and Hans Gatzke have shown that, once war broke out, the German heavy industrial trade associations supported sweeping annexations. However, Georges-Henri Soutou has questioned whether their leaders represented their members, and Bethmann himself was more influenced by relative moderates such as the head of the AEG electricity concern, Walther Rathenau [43; 115; 122].

There is a larger question, irrespective of the degree of business influence, of whether governments went to war for economic reasons. In the Balkans, for example, both the French and Germans encouraged arms sales, and in the pre-1914 period France was gaining the upper hand [36; 41]. What most worried the Central Powers about this development, however, was less the loss of regional export markets than the contribution that it made to Russia's growing *political* ascendancy. And although Austria–Hungary's policy in 1914 of invading and partitioning Serbia was certainly imperialist, its motive was not to win trading or investment opportunities, any more than such considerations influenced Russia's attitude. As for the broader divisions between the Powers, going beyond the Balkan arena, Raymond Poidevin has shown that Franco-German commerce and investment suffered after 1911, but as a consequence of worsening diplomatic relations [40]. And although Berlin embargoed loans to Russia whereas French interests bought huge amounts of Russian Government stock and invested heavily in Russian industry it is questionable whether the economic tie was the mainstay of the Franco-Russian alliance, which was based more on mutual suspicion of Germany. Thus St Petersburg had less need of French money after 1909, but political and military co-operation was strengthened. The Russian Finance and Communications Ministries doubted the benefit of the 1914 railway loan, which was mainly desired by the General Staff and Foreign Ministry for strategic reasons [98; 153]. Finally, trade rivalry between Britain and Germany was lessening as 1914 approached, and did not prevent diplomatic relations from improving. Although Kennedy describes the fundamental source of the antagonism as economic, he qualifies this, as has been seen, by explaining that the problem was not just Germany's faster growth but also its alarming behaviour, and the uses found for the extra resources. We should remember that league tables of Gross National Product were a thing of the future, and that what was thought to matter in estimating military power was not underlying manufacturing potential so much as ready financial reserves and the size and effectiveness of the immediately available armed forces. Russia's economic recovery after 1909 aroused much comment, but what really worried the Germans was its army's re-equipment and accelerating mobilisation [158–9].

Despite the flaws in Lenin's analysis, his portrayal of the Powers as competitive and expansionist does shed light on the origins of the war. To understand why they were so, however, we must consider international as well as domestic conditions. The English writer G. Lowes Dickinson described the international situation as one of 'anarchy' [20], but in fact a major conflict was unlikely to come out of the blue, without a prior build-up of tension. One inhibiting factor, at least in Western Europe, was the high level of economic interdependence, which, according to a widely cited though over-optimistic bestseller by Dickinson's contemporary Norman Angell, made war unprofitable and irrational [35]. In addition, the Powers had a well-established machinery, the 'Concert of Europe', for regulating disputes. Unlike its successors, the League of Nations and the UN, the Concert lacked permanent institutions or a founding document. It consisted of a habit of mind – a willingness by the Powers to seek collective solutions – and a tradition of responding to emergencies by convening conferences of ambassadors or congresses of heads of government. In the pre-war decade conferences met to discuss the First Moroccan Crisis (at Algeciras in 1906) and the First Balkan War (at London in 1912–13).

Recent writers have argued, however, that the Concert was in 'decline' or 'collapse' by 1914 [18; 161]. Austria–Hungary and Germany refused suggestions for a conference during the Bosnian annexation crisis, and did so again after Sarajevo. Although it suited Germany to work with Britain in 1912–13, by 1914 Berlin placed a premium on alliance solidarity, and the Central Powers aimed to achieve their Balkan goals through force rather than via negotiations with the Triple Entente for a mutually acceptable compromise. The Germans had become disillusioned with conferences after finding themselves in a minority at Algeciras. Berchtold concluded during 1913 that the Powers would not impose their will on Serbia and he must pursue unilateral solutions [69]. Yet the breakdown of the Concert was more a symptom of growing tension than a cause. It was a useful face-saving device that could work only when all the Powers wanted it to, and once they were polarised into two alignments it was crippled. Does this mean that, as the Under-Secretary of State in the German Foreign Ministry told the British Ambassador on 1 August 1914, everything was the fault of 'this d — d system of alliances' [4: no. 510]?

Technically, none of the Powers was drawn into war by alliance or entente undertakings. Germany was not obliged to give the blank cheque (as Italy's choice for neutrality demonstrated); Russia had no prior commitment to Serbia. The French could have argued that Russia had mobilised without consultation; the Cabinet in London maintained that it had a free hand. None the less, the diplomatic alignments were central for all concerned. The Austrians would not have acted without Germany's confirmation that it would cover an attack on Serbia, and they may have feared that unless they acted they would lose Berlin's support. The Germans saw Austria–Hungary as their last reliable partner, which might abandon them unless they backed it up: whereas a successful Balkan war could drive a wedge between their enemies. Conversely, the recent strengthening of the Franco-Russian Alliance encouraged Russia to act boldly, and encouraged France to fight rather than desert its partner. If Bethmann hoped to break up the Triple Entente, its members were resolved to stick together.

Moreover, the alliances were taken for granted in the Powers' war plans, and it was the imperatives of the Schlieffen–Moltke Plan that made Germany so rapidly extend the crisis to the west. Similarly, the need to help France quickly forced Russia to aim for speedy operations against Germany, for which it had to make ready as early as possible by implementing its pre-mobilisation measures. The alliances, therefore, help to explain the war plans' bias towards offensive strategies. Jack Snyder has pointed out that as late as 1910 both France and Russia intended to stand on the defensive, but in 1914 Russia's Plan 19 Altered and France's Plan XVII envisaged an immediate invasion of enemy territory. Plan 19 Altered reflected Paris's pressure on its ally for assistance; Plan XVII a growing confidence that the balance was altering to France's and Russia's advantage. Meanwhile Moltke abandoned the option of a first blow to the east, and modified Germany's western plan in part because he expected Britain to intervene. Holland would be spared, so that it could serve as a neutral 'windpipe' through which German trade could circumvent a British blockade, but this modification made it still more vital to secure Liège straightaway. Events soon showed that the faith in the superiority of the offensive was tragically misjudged, and that there was little advantage in attacking first. But while it lasted it strengthened Germany's and Austria–Hungary's incentive to strike before their 'window of opportunity' was closed, and in the crisis itself, once war was seen as possible, it encouraged both sides to scramble to prepare [50: chs 2–4; 51].

The strengthening of the alliances and the adoption of more offensive strategies were linked to the transformation of the arms race into a competition between the two blocs on land. In this form it took off between 1909 and 1912, and intensified in 1912–14. Germany's 1913 law was intended to maintain superiority over France even if Austria–Hungary were distracted by Serbia; with the Three-Year Law and the Great Programme France and Russia counterbalanced it, and reassured each other of their continuing loyalty. Research on intelligence assessment has shown that the two blocs were well informed about their enemies' capabilities [49], and both believed that France and Russia were gaining the advantage. By 1914 they were more evenly matched than in earlier crises, and both could now contemplate military action, this being probably the main respect in which the arms race made war more likely. In theory, a balance of strength should strengthen deterrence, if neither side sees the possibility of victory. But in 1914 *both* did, this resulting partly from faith in the offensive and partly from the balance being a transitory, unstable one, enabling France and Russia to take greater risks than previously while Germany and Austria–Hungary feared losing any chance of victory unless they acted without delay. It is in this sense that the 'balance of power' can most appropriately be blamed for the breakdown of peace [52].

All of these developments help explain why the Balkan confrontation coincided with a general state of tension. It is essential to observe the evolution of the international system as well as its unchanging elements. The Concert had never been able to work unless the Powers wanted it to, and the alliance blocs had existed for a generation. What most destabilised Europe were probably the repeated diplomatic crises, especially from Agadir onwards. Russia's recovery from defeat in Asia would have caused a new round of arms spending anyway, but without the crises the impact would have been less dramatic and unsettling. Once the process of deterioration began, however, it took on a cumulative momentum. The arms race was both caused by international tension and contributed to it, by fuelling public hysteria and aggravating the Central Powers' financial dilemmas. As recently as 1910–11 the Powers had been less distrustful of each other, peaceful solutions did not seem exhausted, the armies were less well prepared, and the advocates of war more isolated and less influential. From then on, however, each crisis added further elements to the combination of circumstances that caused disaster in 1914.

It is the worsening of the international situation, rather than domestic developments, that explains why the Sarajevo crisis was more serious than its predecessors and why war came when it did. That being said, developments on the international and on the domestic levels interacted, and it is hard to disentangle the two. The growing perception of danger made parliaments and finance ministers more willing to increase conscription and defence spending. It weakened the pacifism of the Left, accounting for the otherwise bewildering speed with which political truces were established in 1914. Even if the July Crisis did not embody a counter-revolutionary strategy against the socialists it did demonstrate the power of nationalism. Indeed, according to Bernadotte Schmitt, 'nationalism' (by which he meant the failure of political boundaries to coincide with ethnic ones) was the fundamental cause of the war [23]. The problem with this view is that the Habsburg Monarchy's nationality problems would not have led to general conflict had they not interlocked with the broader European tension. More significant may have been nationalism in the other Great Powers, as evidenced by Russian Pan-Slavism, the French *réveil*, and racist and militarist pressure groups such as the Pan-German League and the *Deutsche Wehrverein* (the German Defence Association, founded in 1912 to lobby for an army increase). However, Sazonov and Bethmann were suspicious of the Pan-Slavs and Pan-Germans, and despite domestic agitation they still restrained Serbia and Austria–Hungary in 1913. The crucial question is not whether extreme nationalists pushed governments into war – they did not – but how far governments chose to act on nationalist agendas.

Part of the problem lies in defining nationalism, a phenomenon that has attracted an explosion of interest from social scientists in recent years. It implies not simply an emotional identification with a nation but a programme of political action on its behalf. But although French politicians described themselves as representatives of the nation, those in St Petersburg and Vienna (and possibly in Berlin) still felt primary loyalty to a dynasty. Moreover, the British, German, and Russian nations had already acquired territorially united and independent states. The French state, admittedly, was incomplete because of the loss of Alsace and Lorraine, but the French did not go to war in order to regain the two provinces. In truth, the Powers were less nation states than empires, controlling subordinate peoples within Europe and outside. The conflicts between them are better described not as nationalist but as imperialist.

Yet if anything 'imperialism' is an even more fraught and difficult term [42]. If its applicability is restricted to extra-European disputes, these, as war approached, might seem to be losing intensity. Britain and Germany could negotiate over Africa and Mesopotamia; France and Germany agreed in February 1914 on spheres of influence in Asia Minor; Russia and Germany reached an understanding in 1910–11 over Persia [90; 100; 155]. This, however, is too narrow a view. The pre-1914 détentes were very limited, as the continuing Anglo-German disagreement over Portuguese colonies shows. The British still regarded the German navy as a threat to their entire world position, while the Russians felt Berlin was challenging their vital interests at the Turkish Straits. Bethmann had not abandoned his colonial aspirations, even if encirclement and the tsarist build-up were more urgent preoccupations. Furthermore, Lenin argued that imperialism existed within Europe as well as outside. If Austrian and Russian ambitions in the Balkans can be equated with French and German ones in Morocco, imperialism can be seen as causing most of the pre-1914 crises, whose destabilising role has already been underlined. And once war had broken out, as Fischer's work and studies of Allied war aims have demonstrated [24; 115; 128], plans for buffer states in Europe and for colonies and naval bases outside it rapidly crystallised.

But despite the undercurrents of imperialism that later surfaced as war aims, in July 1914 both sides were motivated more by insecurity and by fear of others' expansion than by a desire to expand themselves. The threat perceived was less revolution from within (although this played a part) than invasion from outside or, at any rate, the loss of independence, prestige, and bargaining power. At the end of this discussion we return to the leaders of the Powers and their understanding of what war would achieve and what it would be like. Somebody had to pull the trigger. If the international developments discussed above best explain the timing of the outbreak of hostilities, what James Joll christened the 'unspoken assumptions' – the instinctive values and priorities – of the European elites best illuminate those elites' motives for fighting [58]. In fact, these assumptions have left their mark in the documents, but at the time they were so generally accepted as not to need vindication. They require more research.

Joll himself pointed to the influence of Charles Darwin and Friedrich Nietzsche, both of whom were seen as justifying struggle as an inescapable and even desirable characteristic of human existence. Conrad, for example, insisted that war was natural and inevitable, and Bethmann supposed it might bring moral regeneration. Dominic Lieven has suggested that a sense of national honour had been inbred into Russian leaders and is essential to understanding their commitment to Serbia [155]; Avner Offer has examined the notion of honour more generally, relating it to duelling codes in the case of the Continental leaders and to business and professional ethics in London [59]. Modris Eksteins has analysed the aggressive, iconoclastic national mood in Germany and the more conventional, conservative one in Britain [57]. All of this is valuable, with the proviso that there were elements of calculation – particularly of the strategic balance – in 1914 decision-making and not simply internalised 'scripts' that predetermined behavior. Given their responsibility for the fates of historic dynasties and the destinies of millions, the European leaders followed codes that were not quite analogous to those of individuals, foremost among them (and frequently mentioned in the crisis) being their assumptions about what it meant to be a Great Power. Lancelot Farrar has analysed July 1914 as a case of 'limited choice', given these beliefs [112; cf. 50: ch. 8]. Their understanding of Great Powers as expansionist made the German leaders fearful of seeing Russia and France gain the lead. Austria–Hungary felt its power position would be irretrievably compromised if it did nothing about Sarajevo, but so did Russia if it let the Austrians have their way [11]. Both Sazonov and Jagow maintained that firmness would be respected and that resolution rather than concession was the best way to avoid war. Hence in 1914 an issue arose over which neither Vienna nor St Petersburg felt able to yield, and neither Berlin nor Paris insisted on their doing so. Other options existed besides the use of force, but the prevailing assumptions about Great-Power status excluded them.

Conclusion: The Vision of War

Unusually heavy railway traffic is hard to conceal, especially during stifling summer nights when most people would be sleeping with their windows open. Inhabitants of the quarters of the north and south that bordered on the two *ceintures*, the lines that linked up the main-line stations ... must have stirred uneasily in their sleep or have been awakened during *les heures blanches* – three or four in the morning – by the steady rumble of slow-moving trains, a noise that went on right through the night from about the 26th or the 27th... .

The stealthy nightly train movements might have been taken as merely preventive. But the evidence provided by the street scene in Paris on the night of Saturday to Sunday, 1–2 August, indicated quite clearly the steady, irreversible slide from peace into war. The rather impossible Jacques Thibault, totally out of step with the popular mood ... had been surprised to see the doors of Notre-Dame-des-Victoires wide open at midnight, the interior brilliantly lit by hundreds of candles, and the dark figures of young men queuing up outside the confession boxes. When he reached the great clock on the corner of the Quai de l'Horloge and the Boulevard du Palais, it was 1.40 in the morning. The boulevard seemed to shake with a continuous rumble of noise: the sound of hundreds of marching feet, ... [no flowers in the men's rifles], no patriotic songs, just a steady shuffle, as regiment after regiment headed northwards in the direction of the Gare de l'Est and the Gare du Nord. ... Every now and then the steady tramp of men in full campaign equipment and the clip-clop of the patient horses, their heads down, would give way to the heavier rumble of lorries and waggons, of wheeled artillery, horse-drawn, and the sound of civilian cars driven very fast by young soldiers. The noise went on through the entire night, the whole of Monday and all through the night following. ... War had come to Paris and to France.

[12: pp. 136–8]

The short answer to the problem posed in the Introduction is that Balkan events occasioned a world war only because they coincided with a general crisis in Great-Power relations. However, this does not mean that without Sarajevo something else would necessarily have destroyed the peace: previous peaks of general tension (such as in the later 1880s) had passed by without hostilities, as they were to do again during the Soviet–American Cold War. Both the Balkan precipitant and the international context were indispensable to the outcome.

It is also vital to remember that nobody in authority foresaw a war as cataclysmic as 1914–1918 proved to be. Arguably this diminishes the burden of guilt, although none of the European leaders were pacifists, and all were willing to sacrifice their citizens' lives and happiness for the sake of what they deemed to be vital interests. It is true that socialists such as Engels and Jaurès, and conservatives such as Durnovo, had foreseen a desperate struggle that would cause chaos. The most accurate prediction of the military character of the war, Jean de Bloch (Ivan Bloch)'s *The Future of War* [45], foresaw a long drawn-out carnage in which the defence was stronger than the attack, and Bloch's work was widely known at the time. Recent research has questioned whether General Staffs expected victory in a single campaign [121], and Michael Howard has argued that European armies looked less to the Franco-Prussian than to the Russo-Japanese War, which saw trench-fighting, barbed wire and machine guns, and very heavy loss of life. The conclusion drawn, however, was that the offensive would still prevail, and determination would yield victory, at a cost not wholly disproportionate to the likely gains [50: ch. 1]. Most of the pre-1914 futuristic literature envisaged a short war [56], and the political truces at the outbreak of the fighting were established in the expectation that normality would quickly resume [97]. We have a more qualified view than previously, but the generalisation still seems valid that what Lancelot Farrar called the 'short-war illusion' prevailed on both sides [111].

Much of the historical significance of 1914, however, lies in the very fact that the fighting was not over by Christmas. The repercussions included eight million dead, and many times that number traumatised or maimed; as well as worldwide economic dislocation, both hyper-inflation in the 1920s and the Great Depression in the 1930s being more or less direct results. Without the war it is unlikely that the Bolsheviks would have seized power in Russia or that the radical Right would have done so in Italy and Germany. This amounts to saying that the First World War was the indispensable precondition for the Second, from which further global consequences flowed. If the war had ended in six months it would still have had epochal effects, but not, presumably, these.

The question of why the war went on so long even after it turned out to be utterly different from what had expected has been less intensely researched than that of why it broke out at all. Yet the answers are connected. From the autumn of 1914 until 1917 there existed a triple stalemate, at once *military*, in that neither side could achieve a decisive breakthrough, *political*, in that the domestic truces formed in 1914 held firm, and *diplomatic*, in the failure of attempts to negotiate. The bloodshed could be ended neither by victory, nor by revolution, nor by compromise. The Powers were divided not only by the opposing war aims elaborated after hostilities broke out but also by the same basic contradiction that preceded the war: between Germany's efforts to split the Triple Entente, and the Entente's refusal to be divided [24]. The political truces were so solid in part precisely because the July Crisis had helped create the impression in both camps that the struggle was defensive. And the military stalemate was not simply technological, but also reflected the approximate equality (and enormous size) of the two coalitions' resources. Indeed, the same approach to parity between the blocs that had increased the danger in 1914 made it the more likely that if a war did start it would be a long haul. In his *Age of Extremes* Professor Eric Hobsbawm has suggested that it is only with the transformation of 1989–91 that we have finally left the consequences behind us [14]. Yet in the new world we have entered there is little sign of interest in the First World War subsiding, and the riddle of what caused it continues to exert its spell.

Bibliography

This bibliography consists mainly of items cited in the text. Its emphasis is on secondary works rather than on memoirs and documents. Some titles in French and German have been included, but where English translations exist they are given in preference. The first part of the bibliography lists general, comparative, and thematic studies, grouped by topic. The second is arranged by country.

Abbreviations of Periodical Titles

CEH	*Central European History*
EHQ	*European History Quarterly*
GWU	*Geschichte in Wissenschaft und Unterricht*
JCH	*Journal of Contemporary History*
JMH	*Journal of Modern History*
JSS	*Journal of Strategic Studies*
H	*History*
HJ	*The Historical Journal*
HZ	*Historische Zeitschrift*
MGM	*Militärgeschichtliche Mitteilungen*
P&P	*Past and Present*

1. General

(i) Documents

[1] L. Bittner and H. Übersberger (eds), *Österreich-Ungarns Aussenpolitik von der Bosnischen Krise 1908 bis zum Kriegsausbruch 1914*, 9 vols (Vienna, 1930).

[2] Commission de publication des documents relatifs aux origines de la guerre de 1914, *Documents diplomatiques français, 1871–1914*, 41 vols (Paris, 1929–59).

[3]   I. Geiss (ed.), *July 1914: The Outbreak of the First World War. Selected Documents* (New York, 1967). An invaluable one-volume selection, abridged from a German edition.

[4]   G. P. Gooch and H. V. Temperley (eds), *British Documents on the Origins of the War, 1898–1914*, 11 vols (London, 1926–38).

[5]   O. Hoetzsch (ed.), *Die Internationalen Beziehungen im Zeitalter des Imperialismus: Dokumente aus den Archiven der Zarischen und der Provisorischen Regierung, 1878–1917*, Series I, vol. V (German edn, Berlin, 1934).

[6]   *I Documenti Diplomatici Italiani*, 4th series, vol. XII (Rome, 1964).

[7]   J. Lepsius *et al.* (eds), *Die Grosse Politik der europäischen Kabinette, 1871–1914*, 40 vols (Berlin, 1922–7).

[8]   M. Montgelas and W. Schücking (eds), *Outbreak of the World War: German Documents Collected by Karl Kautsky* (New York, 1924).

(ii)   Surveys and Interpretations

[9]   L. Albertini, *The Origins of the War of 1914*, 3 vols (London, 1952–7). The fullest account, and has stood the test of time.

[10]   H. E. Barnes, *The Genesis of the War: An Introduction to the Problem of War Guilt* (New York, 1926). Together with [13] the most influential revisionist account.

[11]   F. R. Bridge, *1914: The Coming of the First World War*, 2nd edn (London, 1988). Cogent brief assessment.

[12]   R. J. Evans and H. Pogge von Strandmann (eds), *The Coming of the First World War* (Oxford, 1988). Some excellent essays.

[13]   S. B. Fay, *The Origins of the World War*, rev. edn, 2 vols (New York, 1930).

[14]   E. J. Hobsbawm, *Age of Extremes: The Short Twentieth Century, 1914–91* (London, 1994).

[15]   J. Joll, *The Origins of the First World War*, 1st and 2nd edns (Harlow, 1984, 1994). The best short synthesis.

[16]   H. W. Koch (ed.), *The Origins of the First World War: Great-Power Rivalry and German War Aims*, 1st and 2nd edns (London and Basingstoke, 1972 and 1984). Translates several contributions to the Fischer controversy.

[17]   J. W. Langdon, *July 1914: The Long Debate, 1918–1990* (Providence, RI and Oxford, 1991). Excellent historiographical survey.

[18]   R. T. B. Langhorne, *The Collapse of the Concert of Europe: International Politics, 1890–1914* (London and Basingstoke, 1981).

[19]   D. E. Lee (ed.), *The Outbreak of the First World War: Who was Responsible?*, rev. edn (Boston, Mass., 1966).

[20]   Lowes Dickinson, G., *The International Anarchy: Europe, 1904–1914* (London, 1926).

[21]   P. E. G. Renouvin, *The Immediate Origins of the War* (New York, 1927).

[22]   B. E. Schmitt, *The Coming of the War, 1914*, 2 vols (New York, 1930). Together with [21], the main early counter-attack against revisionism.

[23]   B. E. Schmitt, *The Origins of the First World War* (London, 1958).

[24]   D. Stevenson, *The First World War and International Politics* (Oxford, 1988).
[25]   A. J. P. Taylor, *The Struggle for Mastery in Europe, 1848–1914* (Oxford, 1954).
[26]   A. J. P. Taylor, *War by Timetable: How the First World War Began* (London, 1969). Argues the thesis in the title.
[27]   L. C. F. Turner, *Origins of the First World War* (London, 1970). Good on strategic aspects.
[28]   K. M. Wilson (ed.), *Decisions for War, 1914* (London, 1995). A valuable update.

(iii)   Socialism and Domestic Political Influences (see also under individual countries)

[29]   M. R. Gordon, 'Domestic Conflict and the Origins of the First World War: the British and the German Cases', *JMH*, **46** (1974), pp. 191–226.
[30]   G. Haupt, *Socialism and the Great War: The Collapse of the Second International* (Oxford, 1972).
[31]   J. Howorth, 'French Workers and German Workers: the Impossibility of Internationalism, 1900–1914', *EHQ*, **15** (1985), pp. 71–97. Looks at trade unionists rather than socialists.
[32]   J. Joll, *The Second International, 1889–1914*, new edn (London, 1974).
[33]   A. J. Mayer, 'Domestic Causes of the First World War', in L. Krieger and F. Stern (eds), *The Responsibility of Power: Historical Essays in Honour of Hajo Holborn* (New York, 1967), pp. 286–300.
[34]   A. J. Mayer, *The Persistence of the Old Regime: Europe to the Great War* (London, 1981).

(iv)   The International Economy and Imperialism

[35]   N. Angell, *The Great Illusion: A Study of the Relation of Military Power to Political Advantage* (London, 1909).
[36]   H. Feis, *Europe – The World's Banker, 1870–1914* (repr., New York, 1964). Pioneering study of international finance.
[37]   E. J. Hobsbawm, *The Age of Empire, 1875–1914* (London, 1987). A sophisticated Marxist analysis.
[38]   V. I. Lenin, *Imperialism, the Highest Stage of Capitalism: A Popular Outline* (repr., Beijing, 1975).
[39]   A. Offer, *The First World War: An Agrarian Interpretation* (Oxford, 1989). Stimulating reappraisal, discussing British and German dependence on overseas trade.
[40]   R. Poidevin, *Les relations économiques et financières entre la France et l'Allemagne de 1898 à 1914* (Paris, 1969).
[41]   R. Poidevin, 'Fabricants d'armes et relations internationales au début du xxe siècle', *Relations internationales*, **1** (1974), pp. 39–56.

[42]   A. Porter, *European Imperialism, 1860–1914* (Basingstoke, 1994).

[43]   G.-H. Soutou, *L'Or et le sang: les buts de guerre économiques de la Première Guerre mondiale* (Paris, 1989).

[44]   C. Strikwerda, 'The Troubled Origins of European Economic Integration: International Iron and Steel and Labor Migration in the Era of World War I', *American Historical Review*, **98** (1993), 1106–41.

(v)   Armaments, Militarism, and Strategy

[45]   J. de Bloch, *The Future of War in its Technical, Economic and Political Relations* (Boston, Mass., 1899).

[46]   A. Bucholz, *Moltke, Schlieffen, and Prussian War Planning* (New York, 1991). Absorbing analysis.

[47]   P. M. Kennedy (ed.), *The War Plans of the Great Powers, 1880–1914* (London, 1979). A series of useful essays.

[48]   J. S. Levy, T. J. Christensen and M. Trachtenberg, 'Mobilization and Inadvertence in the July Crisis', *International Security*, **16** (1991), pp. 189–203.

[49]   E. R. May (ed.), *Knowing One's Enemies: Intelligence Assessment before the World Wars* (Princeton, N.J., 1984). Fascinating material.

[50]   S. E. Miller (ed.), *Military Strategy and the Origins of the First World War*, rev. edn (Princeton, N.J., 1991). Essays, mostly by political scientists, from the journal *International Security*.

[51]   J. Snyder, *The Ideology of the Offensive: Military Decision-Making and the Disasters of 1914* (Ithaca, N.Y., 1984).

[52]   D. Stevenson, *Armaments and the Coming of War: Europe, 1904–1914* (Oxford, 1996). The interaction between armaments and diplomacy.

[53]   M. Trachtenberg, 'The Coming of the First World War: A Reassessment', in his *History and Strategy* (Princeton, N.J., 1991), pp. 47–99. Criticises the notion of 'inadvertent' war.

[54]   L. C. F. Turner, 'The Role of the General Staffs in July 1914', *Australian Journal of Politics and History*, **11** (1965), pp. 305–23. Downplays military influence.

[55]   S. R. Williamson, *The Politics of Grand Strategy: Britain and France Prepare for War, 1904–1914* (Cambridge, Mass., 1969). Definitive on Entente war planning.

(vi)   Cultural Factors: The Mood of 1914

[56]   I. F. Clarke, *Voices Prophesying War, 1763–1984* (London, 1966). Fictional prefigurations of the war.

[57]   M. Eksteins, *Rites of Spring: The Great War and the Birth of the Modern Age* (London, 1989). Cultural history of the most imaginative kind.

[58]   J. Joll, '1914: The Unspoken Assumptions', in [16], 1st edn, pp. 307–28.
       Pointed to a new field of research.
[59]   A. Offer, 'Going to War in 1914: a Matter of Honour?', *Politics & Society*,
       23 (1995), pp. 213–41. Develops the unspoken assumptions theme.
[60]   D. Pick, *War Machine: The Rationalisation of Slaughter in the Modern Age*
       (New Haven, Conn., and London, 1993). Includes the pre-1914 period.

2.   Individual Countries

(i)   Austria–Hungary

[61]   F. R. Bridge, *From Sadowa to Sarajevo: The Foreign Policy of Austria–
       Hungary, 1866–1914* (London, 1972). With valuable appended
       documents.
[62]   F. R. Bridge, *The Habsburg Monarchy among the Great Powers, 1815–1918*
       (New York, Oxford, and Munich, 1990). Updated version of [61].
[63]   F. Conrad von Hötzendorf, *Aus Meiner Dienstzeit, 1906–1918*, 5 vols
       (Vienna, 1921–5).
[64]   K. Hitchins, 'The Nationality Problem in Hungary: István Tisza and the
       Rumanian National Party, 1910–1914', *Journal of Modern History*, **15**
       (1981), pp. 619–51.
[65]   J. Leslie, 'The Antecedents of Austria-Hungary's War Aims: Policies and
       Policy-Making in Vienna and Budapest before and during 1914', *Wiener
       Beiträge zur Geschichte der Neuzeit*, **20** (1993), pp. 307–94. Important new
       information.
[66]   G. E. Rothenberg, *The Army of Francis Joseph* (West Lafayette, Ind., 1976).
[67]   N. Stone, 'Moltke–Conrad: Relations between the Austro-Hungarian
       and German General Staffs, 1909–1914', *HJ*, **9** (1966), pp. 201–28.
[68]   N. Stone, 'Hungary and the Crisis of July 1914', *JCH*, **1** (1966),
       pp. 153–70.
[69]   S. R. Williamson, 'Vienna and July 1914: the Origins of the Great War
       Once More', in [70], pp. 8–36. Excellent summary.
[70]   S. R. Williamson and P. Pastor (eds), *Essays on World War I: Origins and
       Prisoners of War* (New York, 1983).
[71]   S. R. Williamson, *Austria–Hungary and the Origins of the First World War*
       (Basingstoke, 1991). With [61], the best general account.

(ii)   Britain and Anglo-German Relations

[72]   W. S. Churchill, *The World Crisis, 1911–1914* (London, 1923). A classic
       that still repays reading.
[73]   R. J. Crampton, *The Hollow Detente: Anglo-German Relations in the Balkans,
       1911–1914* (London, 1980). The limits to pre-war rapprochement.

[74] M. Ekstein, 'Sir Edward Grey and Imperial Germany in 1914', *JCH*, **6** (1971), pp. 121–31. Suggests Grey misread the situation in Berlin.

[75] D. French, 'The Edwardian Crisis and the Origins of the First World War', *International History Review*, **4** (1982), pp. 207–21. Questions the connection between foreign policy and domestic unrest.

[76] A. Friedberg, *The Weary Titan: Britain and the Experience of Relative Decline, 1895–1905* (Princeton, N.J., 1988).

[77] B. B. Gilbert, 'Pacifist to Interventionist: David Lloyd George in 1911 and 1914. Was Belgium an Issue?', *HJ*, **28** (1985), pp. 863–85. Why Lloyd George supported intervention.

[78] J. Gooch, *The Plans of War: The General Staff and British Military Strategy, 1900–1916* (London, 1974).

[79] E. Grey, *Twenty-Five Years, 1892–1916*, 2 vols (London, 1925).

[80] C. Hazlehurst, *Politicians at War, July 1914 to May 1915: A Prologue to the Triumph of Lloyd George* (London, 1971). Analyses the Cabinet debates.

[81] F. H. Hinsley (ed.), *British Foreign Policy under Sir Edward Grey* (Cambridge, 1977). Essays on all aspects of British diplomacy.

[82] P. M. Kennedy, *The Rise of the Anglo-German Antagonism, 1860–1914* (London, 1980). Comprehensive analysis.

[83] R. T. B. Langhorne, 'The Naval Question in Anglo-German Relations, 1912–1914', *HJ*, **14** (1971), pp. 359–70.

[84] R. T. B. Langhorne, 'Anglo-German Negotiations Concerning the Future of the Portuguese Colonies, 1911–1914', *HJ*, **16** (1973), 361–87.

[85] D. Lloyd George, *War Memoirs*, 6 vols (London, 1933–6).

[86] J. H. Maurer, 'Churchill's Naval Holiday: Arms Control and the Anglo-German Naval Race, 1912–1914,', *JSS*, **15** (1992), pp. 102–27.

[87] A. J. A. Morris, *Radicalism against War, 1906–1914: The Advocacy of Peace and Retrenchment* (Totowa, N. J., 1972).

[88] A. J. A. Morris, *The Scaremongers: The Advocacy of War and Rearmament, 1896–1914* (London, 1984).

[89] K. G. Robbins, *Sir Edward Grey* (London, 1971).

[90] Z. S. Steiner, *Britain and the Origins of the First World War* (London and Basingstoke, 1977). Excellent one-volume introduction.

[91] S. J. Valone, ' "There Must be Some Misunderstanding": Sir Edward Grey's Diplomacy of August 1, 1914', *Journal of British Studies*, **27** (1988), pp. 405–24.

[92] K. M. Wilson, 'The British Cabinet's Decision for War, 2 August 1914', *British Journal of International Studies*, **1** (1975), 148–59. Stresses domestic political considerations.

[93] K. M. Wilson, 'Imperial Interests in the British Decision for War, 1914: the Defence of India in Asia', *Review of International Studies*, **10** (1984), pp. 189–203.

[94] K. M. Wilson, *The Policy of the Entente: Essays on the Determinants of British Foreign Policy, 1904–1914* (Cambridge, 1985).

[95] T. Wilson, 'Britain's "Moral Commitment" to France in August 1914', *H*, **64** (1979), pp. 80–90.

[96] H. F. Young, 'The Misunderstanding of August 1, 1914', *JMH*, **48** (1976), pp. 644–65.

(iii)   France and the Franco-Russian Alliance

[97]   J.-J. Becker, *1914: Comment les Français sont entrés dans la guerre* (Paris, 1977). The best study of public opinion anywhere.

[98]   R. Girault, *Emprunts russes et investissements français en Russie, 1887–1914* (Paris, 1973). The Franco-Russian financial relationship.

[99]   M. B. Hayne, *The French Foreign Office and the Origins of the First World War, 1898–1914* (Oxford, 1993). Important on Paléologue.

[100]   J. F. V. Keiger, *France and the Origins of the First World War* (London and Basingstoke, 1983). The best introduction.

[101]   G. Krumeich, *Armaments and Politics in France on the Eve of the First World War: The Introduction of Three-Year Conscription, 1913–1914* (Leamington Spa, 1984). Incisive on French rearmament.

[102]   R. N. L. Poincaré, *Au Service de la France: Neuf années de souvenirs*, 10 vols (Paris, 1926–33).

[103]   D. W. Spring, 'Russia and the Franco-Russian Alliance, 1905–1914: Dependence or Interdependence?', *Slavonic and East European Review*, **66** (1988), pp. 565–92. Important discussion.

[104]   J. Stengers, '1914: the Safety of Cyphers and the Outbreak of the First World War', in C. M. Andrew and J. Noakes (eds), *Intelligence and International Relations, 1900–1945* (Exeter, 1987), pp. 29–48.

(iv)   Germany: Fischer and his Critics

[105]   V. R. Berghahn, *Germany and the Approach of War in 1914*, 2nd edn (Basingstoke, 1993). The best one-volume account, with a valuable introductory essay.

[106]   A. Blänsdorff, 'Der Weg der Riezler-Tagebücher. Zur Kontroverse über die Echtheit der Tagebücher Kurt Riezlers', *GWU*, **35** (1984), pp. 651–84. Defends the diaries against their critics.

[107]   R. J. B. Bosworth, *Explaining Auschwitz and Hiroshima: History Writing and the Second World War, 1945–1990* (London, 1993). Despite the title, Chapter 3 is highly relevant on Fischer.

[108]   D. K. Buse, 'Party Leadership and Mechanisms of Unity: the Crisis of German Social Democracy Reconsidered, 1910–1914', *JMH*, **62** (1990), pp. 477–502. The SPD's unity and radicalisation.

[109]   K. D. Erdmann, 'Zur Beurteilung Bethmann Hollwegs', *GWU*, **15** (1964), pp. 525–40. The first use of the Riezler diaries.

[110]   K. D. Erdmann, 'Zur Echtheit der Tagebücher Kurt Riezlers: eine Antikritik', *HZ*, **136** (1983), pp. 371–402. A reply to [140].

[111]   L. L. Farrar, Jr, *The Short-War Illusion: German Policy, Strategy, and Domestic Affairs, August–December 1914* (Santa Barbara, Cal., 1973).

[112]   L. L. Farrar, Jr, *Arrogance and Anxiety: The Ambivalence of German Power, 1848–1914* (Iowa City, 1981). Interprets July 1914 as 'limited choice'.

[113]   N. Ferguson, 'Germany and the Origins of the First World War: New Perspectives', *HJ*, **35** (1992), pp. 725–52. Surveys recent literature.

[114] N. Ferguson, 'Public Finance and National Security: the Domestic Origins of the First World War Revisited', *P&P*, **142** (1994), pp. 141–68. Of major importance.

[115] F. Fischer, *Germany's Aims in the First World War* (London, 1967).

[116] F. Fischer, *World Power or Decline: The Controversy over Germany's Aims in the First World War* (London, 1975).

[117] F. Fischer, *War of Illusions: German Policies from 1911 to 1914* (London, 1975).

[118] F. Fischer, *Wir sind nicht hineingeschlittert. Das Staatsgeheimnis um die Riezler-Tagebücher. Eine Streitschrift* (Hamburg, 1983). An attack on the Riezler diaries and a riposte against Fischer's critics.

[119] F. Fischer, 'Twenty-Five Years Later: Looking Back at the "Fischer Controversy" and its Consequences', *CEH*, **21** (1988), pp. 207–23. A helpful retrospective.

[120] S. Förster, *Der Doppelte Militarismus: die Deutsche Heeresrüstung zwischen Status-Quo-Sicherung und Aggression, 1890–1913* (Stuttgart, 1985). Fundamental on armaments.

[121] S. Förster, 'Der deutsche Generalstab und die Illusion des kurzen Krieges, 1871–1914. Metakritik eines Mythos', *MGM*, **54** (1995), no. I, pp. 61–95. Questions whether the General Staff expected a short war.

[122] H. W. Gatzke, *Germany's Drive to the West: A Study of Western War Aims during the First World War* (Baltimore, Md, 1950).

[123] D. Groh, 'The "Unpatriotic Socialists" and the State', *JCH*, **1** (1966), pp. 151–77. Summarises a major monograph on the SPD.

[124] A. Hillgruber, 'Riezlers Theorie des Kalkulierten Risikos und Bethmann Hollwegs Politische Konzeptionen in der Julikrise, 1914', *HZ*, **202** (1966), pp. 333–51. The 'calculated risk' interpretation of Bethmann's policy.

[125] I. V. Hull, *The Entourage of Kaiser Wilhelm II, 1888–1918* (Cambridge, 1982).

[126] W. Jäger, *Historische Forschung und Politische Kultur in Deutschland: die Debatte 1914–1980 über den Ausbruch des Ersten Weltkrieges* (Göttingen, 1984). Places the Fischer controversy in its context.

[127] K. F. Jarausch, 'The Illusion of Limited War: Bethmann Hollweg's Calculated Risk in July 1914', *CEH*, **2** (1969), pp. 48–76. Best statement in English of the 'calculated risk' interpretation.

[128] K. H. Jarausch, *The Enigmatic Chancellor: Bethmann Hollweg and the Hubris of Imperial Germany* (New Haven, Conn., 1973).

[129] D. E. Kaiser, 'Germany and the Origins of the First World War', *JMH*, **55** (1983), pp. 442–74. Criticises the 'primacy of domestic policy' school.

[130] W. J. Mommsen, 'Domestic Factors in German Policy before 1914', *CEH*, **6** (1973), pp. 3–43.

[131] W. J. Mommsen, 'The Topos of Inevitable War in Germany in the Decade before 1914', in V. R. Berghahn and M. Kitchen (eds), *Germany in the Age of Total War* (London, 1981).

[132] J. A. Moses, *The Politics of Illusion: The Fischer Controversy in German Historiography* (London, 1975).

[133]   K. Riezler, *Tagebücher, Aufsätze, Dokumente*, ed. K. D. Erdmann (Göttingen, 1972). See [106], [110], [118], [140].

[134]   G. A. Ritter, *The Schlieffen Plan: Critique of a Myth* (London, 1958). Includes key military documents.

[135]   G. A. Ritter, 'Eine neue Kriegsschuldthese? Zu Fritz Fischers Buch "Griff nach der Weltmacht"', *HZ*, **194** (1962), pp. 646–68.

[136]   G. A. Ritter, *The Sword and the Scepter: The Problem of Militarism in German History*, vol. II (Coral Gables, Fla., 1970).

[137]   J. C. G. Röhl, 'Admiral von Müller and the Approach of War, 1911–1914', *HJ*, **12** (1969), pp. 651–73. Important for the War Council.

[138]   J. C. G. Röhl, 'An der Schwelle zum Weltkrieg: eine Dokumentation über den Kriegsrat vom 8. Dezember 1912', *MGM* (1977), 77–134. All the War Council documentation.

[139]   G. Schöllgen, *Escape into War? The Foreign Policy of Imperial Germany* (Oxford, New York, and Munich, 1990). Restatements by Fischer and others.

[140]   B. Sösemann, 'Die Tagebücher Kurt Riezlers: Untersuchungen zu ihrer Echtheit und Edition', *HZ*, **236** (1983), pp. 327–69. A damaging critique of the Riezler diaries' authenticity.

[141]   U. Trumpener, 'War Premeditated? German Intelligence Operations in July 1914', *CEH*, **9** (1976), pp. 58–85. Includes important new evidence.

[142]   V. Ullrich, 'Das deutsche Kalkül in der Julikrise 1914 und die Frage der englischen Neutralität', *GWU*, **34** (1983), pp. 79–97. German estimates of the likelihood of British neutrality.

[143]   V. Ullrich, *Kriegsalltag: Hamburg im Ersten Weltkrieg* (Cologne, 1982). The experience of one German city.

[144]   H.-U. Wehler, *The German Empire, 1871–1918* (Leamington Spa, 1985). Emphatic on the primacy of domestic factors.

(v)   Italy

[145]   R. J. B. Bosworth, *Italy and the Approach of the First World War* (London, 1983). The best introduction.

[146]   J. Gooch, *Army, State, and Society in Italy, 1870–1915* (Basingstoke, 1989).

[147]   C. J. Lowe and F. Marzari, *Italian Foreign Policy, 1870–1940* (London, 1975).

[148]   M. Palumbo, 'German–Italian Military Relations on the Eve of World War I', *CEH*, **12** (1979), pp. 343–71.

(vi)   The Ottoman Empire

[149]   M. Kent (ed.), *The Great Powers and the End of the Ottoman Empire* (London, 1984). The best survey.

[150]   R. J. Kerner, 'The Mission of Liman von Sanders', *Slavonic Review*, **6** (1927), pp. 12–27, 344–63, 543–60, and **7** (1982), pp. 90–112.

(vii)   *Russia*

[151]   W. C. Fuller, *Strategy and Power in Russia, 1600–1914* (New York, 1992). Helpful on the reorganisation of 1910.

[152]   P. W. Gatrell, *Government, Industry, and Rearmament in Russia, 1900–1914: The Last Argument of Tsarism* (Cambridge, 1994). Excellent on the military build-up.

[153]   D. Geyer, *Russian Imperialism: The Interaction of Domestic and Foreign Policy, 1860–1914* (Leamington Spa, 1987). Very valuable on the roots of Russian policy.

[154]   B. Jelavich, *Russia's Balkan Entanglements, 1806–1914* (Cambridge, 1991). Analyses Russia's commitment to Serbia.

[155]   D. C. B. Lieven, *Russia and the Origins of the First World War* (Basingstoke, 1983). A searching introduction.

[156]   D. C. B. Lieven, *Nicholas II: Emperor of all the Russias* (London, 1993).

[157]   H. Rogger, 'Russia in 1914', *JCH*, **1/4** (1966), pp. 95–119.

[158]   R. Ropponen, *Die Kraft Russlands: Wie Beurteilte die Politische und die Militärische Führung der Europäischen Grossmächte in der Zeit von 1905 bis 1914 die Kraft Russlands?* (Helsinki, 1968). How others assessed Russia.

[159]   W. C. Wohlforth, 'The Perception of Power: Russia in the Pre-1914 Balance', *World Politics*, **39** (1987), pp. 353–81. Summarises [158].

(viii)   *Serbia, the Balkans, and Sarajevo*

[160]   M. S. Anderson, *The Eastern Question, 1774–1923: A Study in International Relations* (London and Basingstoke, 1966). Provides the background.

[161]   R. J. Crampton, 'The Decline of the Concert of Europe in the Balkans, 1913–1914', *Slavonic and East European Review*, **52** (1974), pp. 393–419. Important on the Concert.

[162]   V. Dedijer, *The Road to Sarajevo* (New York, 1966). The standard work.

[163]   D. Mackenzie, *Apis: The Congenial Conspirator – The Life of Colonel Dragutin T. Dimitrijević* (New York, 1989).

[164]   N. Malcolm, *Bosnia: A Short History* (London and Basingstoke, 1994). A readable introduction.

[165]   J. Remak, *Sarajevo: The Story of a Political Murder* (London, 1959).

Index

Bloch, Ivan, 56
Boers, 36
Bolsheviks, 39, 45, 57
Bosnia-Herzegovina, xi, 2, 3, 4
    Bosnia Crisis (1908–9), xi, 4, 5, 13,
        16, 21, 24, 48
Britain, x, xi, xii, 2, 5, 8–11, 13, 18, 24,
    27–38, 42, 43, 45, 46, 49, 50, 52,
    55
British Expeditionary Force (BEF),
    33, 37, 38, 42
Bucharest, Treaty of (1913), xi
Bulgaria, xi, 6
business interests, 44, 46, 47; see also
    arms sales; capitalism; economic
    explanations of war origins

Cambon, Paul, xi, 33, 35
capitalism, 44, 46
Carnet B, 26, 46
CGT, 26, 45
Channel, English, 33
Churchill, Winston, 34, 36, 37, 38, 39,
    43, 44
coloured books, 39
commercial relations, 41, 46, 47, 48
    Austro-Hungarian, 5
    British, 35, 36, 37, 47
    French, 47
    German, 10, 22, 31, 35, 36, 37, 47
    Russian, 21, 22
    Serbian, 5
concentration, 22
Concert of Europe, 48, 49, 50
Conrad von Hötzendorf, Franz, 5, 6,
    7, 8, 30, 39, 53
Creditanstalt, 46
Croatia, Croats, 3, 4
cultural explanations of war origins,
    41, 53; see also honour;
    nationalism; unspoken
    assumptions
Czechs, 4

Dardanelles, see Straits, Turkish
Darwin, Charles, 53
Deutsche Wehrverein, 51
Dickinson, G. Lowes, 48

Dimitrijević, Colonel ('Apis'), 3
documents, diplomatic, 39, 40, 41
Dreadnought, HMS, xi, 13
    dreadnought battleships, 13, 14, 36,
        44
Durnovo, Peter, 45, 56

Eastern Question, x, 20
economic explanations of war origins,
    see arms sales; capitalism;
    commercial relations; financial
    relations; imperialism; Lenin
Eksteins, Modris, 53
encirclement, 13, 52
Engels, Friedrich, 45, 56
ententes
    Anglo-French, xi, 13, 32, 35, 45
    Anglo-Russian, 13, 32, 35, 45
    Triple, 2, 5, 11, 12, 16, 18, 19, 20,
        26, 30, 43, 48, 49, 57
Essen, 46

Falkenhayn, Erich von, 30
Farrar, Lancelot, 53, 57
Fashoda Crisis, x
Fay, Sidney, 41, 52
financial relations
    France, xii, 5, 47
    Germany, 22, 47
    Russia, xii, 5, 22, 47
    Serbia, 5
Fischer, Fritz, 10, 11, 12, 16, 18, 19,
    28, 29, 31, 41, 43, 47
Flucht nach vorn ['flight forward'], 12,
    46
France, x, xi, xii, 2, 5, 7, 8, 9, 11, 12,
    13, 15, 16, 20, 24–35, 37, 38, 40,
    42–52, 54
Franco-Prussian War, 34, 56
Frankfurt, Treaty of (1871), x
Franz Ferdinand, Archduke, 2, 3, 6
Franz Joseph (Austrian Emperor), 4, 6

Gatzke, Hans, 46
General Staffs
    Austro-Hungarian, 5
    German, 7, 17, 51
    Russian, 23, 47

George V (British King), 37
Germany, x, xi, xii, 2, 5–17, 19, 20, 21,
    22, 23, 25, 26, 28–32, 35–50, 52,
    53, 54, 57
Goremykin, Ivan, 22
Great Programme, *see* army bills
    (Russian)
Greece, xi
Grey, Sir Edward, xi, 14, 29, 31, 33, 34,
    35, 36, 37, 38, 39, 43, 44

Habsburgs, 2, 5, 19, 32
Helgoland, 16
Hobsbawm, Eric, 57
Hohenzollerns, 19, 45
Honour, National, 53
Howard, Michael, 56
Hoyos, Count, 6, 8, 18
Hungary, 4, 6

imperialism, 46, 47, 52, 53
India, 35
intelligence, military, 3, 23, 41, 50
International Socialist Bureau, 44, 45
Ireland, 33, 38, 46
Italy, x, xi, xii, 2, 5, 7, 13, 16, 21, 32,
    49, 57

Jagow, Gottlieb von, 16, 18, 23, 29, 54
Japan, x, 24
Janushkevich, General, 23
Jaurès, Jean, 26, 56
Jelavich, Barbara, 21
Joffre, Joseph, 25, 26, 30
Joll, James, 42, 53

Kautsky, Karl, 39
Kennedy, Paul, 35, 37, 47
Kiel Canal, 16, 17
Kiev, 22
Kokovtsov, Vladimir, 22
Kriegsgefahrzustand, xii, 28, 30
Krupp, 18, 46

Langdon, John, 42
Lenin, Vladimir Ilyich, 46, 52
Levy, Jack, 29
Liberal Party (Britain), 34, 35, 44

Libya, 16, 32
Lichnowsky, Prince, 29
Liège, 15, 30, 50
Lieven, Dominic, 53
Liman von Sanders, General, xi, 14,
    22, 23
Lloyd George, David, 9, 29, 34, 43, 44
London, 34, 37
London Conference (1912–13), xi, 48
London, Treaty of (1839), 32, 33
Luxemburg, xii, 9

Mansion House speech, 29
Marx, Karl, 45
Mayer, Arno, 12
Mediterranean Sea, 33
Mesopotamia, 52
'misunderstanding' (Anglo-German,
    1 August 1914), xii, 31, 34, 35
Mitteleuropa, 10, 11, 31
mobilization, 22
    Austro-Hungarian, xii
    French, 55, 56
    German, 22, 23, 25, 28, 30
    Russian, xii, 8, 18, 20, 22, 23, 25, 26,
        28, 30, 42, 48
    Serbian, xii
Moltke the Younger, Helmuth von, 9,
    11, 15, 16, 17, 18, 23, 30, 31, 42,
    43, 49, 50
Mommsen, Wolfgang, 17
Montenegro, xi, 6, 7, 21
Moroccan Crisis, First (1905–6), xxi,
    13, 16, 29, 48
Moroccan Crisis, Second (1911), xi,
    14, 16, 25, 29

Napoleon I (French Emperor), 37
nationalism, 25, 41, 46, 51, 52
naval conversations (Anglo-Russian,
    1914), xii, 14, 18, 29
naval holiday, 36
navies
    British, xi, 13, 14, 24, 32, 33, 36, 37,
        38
    French, 33
    German, x, xi, 12, 13, 14, 17, 36, 45,
        52

70